The ELSA
Trainers' Manual

www.teachingexpertise.com/teachtoinspire

The ELSA Trainers' Manual

Sheila Burton

We are grateful to Hampshire Educational Psychology Service
for generously making the materials developed within the
service available for this publication.

Routledge
Taylor & Francis Group
LONDON AND NEW YORK

First published 2009 by Optimus Education: a division of Optimus Professional Publishing Ltd.

Published 2018 by Routledge
711 Third Avenue, New York, NY 10017, USA
2 Park Square, Milton Park, Abingdon, Oxon OX14 4RN

Routledge is an imprint of the Taylor & Francis Group, an informa business

ISBN 9781138090514 (pbk)

A CD-ROM and a DVD are attached to the inside front cover and are integral parts of this publication.

Contents

Supplementary Training   341

References   361

Use of the CD-ROM and DVD

Many Teach to Inspire publications include CD-ROMs to support the purchaser in the delivery of the training or teaching activities. These may include any of the following file formats:

- PDFs requiring Acrobat v.3.
- Microsoft Word files.
- Microsoft PowerPoint files.
- Video clips which can be played by Windows Media Player.
- If games are included the software required is provided on the CD-ROM.

All material on the accompanying CD-ROM can be printed by the purchaser/user of the book. This includes library copies. Some of this material is also printed in the book and can be photocopied but this will restrict it to the black and white/greyscale version when there might be a colour version on the CD-ROM.

The CD-ROM itself must not be reproduced or copied in its entirety for use by others without permission from the publisher.

All material on the CD-ROM is © Burton 2009

Symbol Key

 This symbol indicates a page that can be photocopied from the book or printed from the PDF file on the CD-ROM.

 This symbol indicates a page that can be photocopied from the book or modified and printed from the Word file on the CD-ROM.

Use of the DVD

A DVD is provided of a training session delivered to ELSAs by the author. This includes explanation of the purpose behind using puppets and various ideas for how to use them. It is for use on Day 3 of the programme.

The DVD must not be reproduced or copied for use by others without permission from the publisher.

Acknowledgements

I would like to acknowledge the contribution of past and present members of the Hampshire Educational Psychology Service (2004-2009) to implementation of the ELSA project across the county. Some psychologists have contributed directly to the training. Many psychologists facilitate ELSA supervision groups. Most psychologists have contact with ELSAs in the schools they support. Without the administrative assistance of our excellent support officers this work would not have been possible. Special thanks to Fliss Dickinson, County Services Manager (SEN and Specialist Teacher Advisors), Hampshire Children's Services Department, for her continuing interest and support. Whether your involvement has been considerable or peripheral, your support is valued. Thank you.

Sheila

Educational Psychologists		Psychology Research Associates
Julia Alfano	Kate Jenkins	Jayne Beresford
Anne Atkinson	Kathy Johnston	Cara Osborne
Jackie Batchelor	Helen Jones	Maria Traill
Susie Bayles	Gay Keegan	Amy Warhurst
Bernadette Begley	Hayley Lan	
Jo Birbeck	Judith Lee	Assistant Psychologists
Jess Bradley	Jeanie Low-Ying	Chloe Allen
John Burrell	Helen Mabey	Nicola Rabbitts
Cathy Byron	Colin Macpherson	Zoe Reavill
David Byron	Lucy Manger	Tom Sargeant
Nicola Boobyer	Lisa McSpadden	
Bob Carabine	Joanne Moran	Support Officers
Marina Chan-Pensley	Janet Morton	Louise Arnold
Charlotte Crowther	Roger Norgate	Sue Bate
Zoe Collins	Sue Peters	Carrie Blythe
Tim Cooke	Nicky Phillips	Andrea Bruce
Anna Cox	Julia Powell	Andrea Carr
Jo Currie	Sam Poynter	Tracy Carter
Cheryl Curtis	Neal Ridley	Barbara Chandler
Anita Davis	Kate Ripley	Yvonne Colville
Anne Duggan	Hilary Robbins	Trish Dores
Gordon Edgar	Hannah Sandison	Sue Fodeh
Caroline Feltham-King	Sue Sheppard	Caroline Goodman
Jacki Fiander	Gillian Shotton	Gill Goodman
Rachael Gass	Paul Skinner	Paula Green
Barbara Gessler	Dawn Slattery	Sue Hilden
Emma Gibbs	Jane Sleight	Sam Hill
Sue Gibson	Veronica Steele	Elaine Howells
Kate Hancock	Phil Stringer	Jane Ingram
Joyce Harrison	Dan Taylor	Sophie Isherwood
Hilary Hickmore	Chris Travell	Jackie Patten
David Hogg	Cliff Turner	Wendy Steel
Sarah Holland	Kirsty Ward	Sue Thirlby
Jeni Hooper	Alison Watson	Beverley Torkington
Phil Horton	Lesley Webster	Sue Turner
Lisa Hobkirk	Sarah Wright	Helen Tustin
Marion Hobbs	Rebecca Young	Diane Sambrook
Helena Hoyos		Denise Uren
Cerian Hughes		Bev Uphill
Sue Ingham		Joanne Wright

Supplementary Materials from Hampshire – ELSAs in Action!

A DVD of Hampshire Emotional Literacy Support Assistants in action has been produced for training and promotional purposes. It features ELSAs working with infant, junior and secondary pupils and includes individual and group sessions. The ELSAs speak about their role, and a primary headteacher and secondary assistant headteacher talk about the impact of the ELSA project on their schools. The project co-ordinator talks about the rationale of ELSA work and the outcomes for pupils.

This DVD was made in response to requests by ELSAs in training to be able to see film of experienced colleagues in action. It highlights some of the key elements of a well-planned session. This will be a useful resource for local authorities establishing ELSA work in their own area, and for schools wishing to raise staff awareness of the ELSA role.

A copy of the DVD 'ELSAs in Action' (duration approximately 60 minutes) is available at a cost of £25 (inc p+p) + VAT, from Hampshire Educational Psychology Service, Winchester Local Office, Clarendon House, Monarch Way, Winchester, SO22 5PW.

Foreword

I am pleased to be writing the foreword to the Emotional Literacy Support Assistant (ELSA) Trainers' Manual. In working to promote the emotional wellbeing of children and young people, the role of the ELSA in Hampshire schools has rapidly become established as an invaluable resource.

Classroom Assistants, or Learning Support Assistants (LSAs) as they are known in Hampshire, have become a fact of life in schools across the United Kingdom. As educational psychologists routinely working in schools, we regularly work with LSAs. We are only too aware of the valuable resource that they represent and the commitment and enthusiasm that they bring to their work. We also recognise the thirst that LSAs have to develop both their understanding of children and young people and also their skills in intervening to make a positive difference. We know, too, that developing understanding and skills cannot and should not be left to chance.

Whilst it might go without saying that a central purpose of effective parenting and effective schooling is to promote emotional development and wellbeing, we also know that this cannot be left to chance either. Indeed, one does not have to look far to find arguments about the extent to which a school can balance a focus on academic attainment with a regard for wellbeing. Nor does one have to look far to find concerns about the challenges to wellbeing that children face as they grow up in the twenty-first century, as highlighted most recently by 'The Good Childhood Inquiry'.

These matters, as Sheila Burton recognises in Part One of this manual, are at the heart of the initiative to develop the skills of LSAs so that they can fulfill the role of an Emotional Literacy Support Assistant.

The ELSA programme draws together many of the elements that we know can make a difference for children and young people and for the adults that care for and work with them. It is also a testimony to Sheila's commitment and enthusiasm to promoting wellbeing, and to her understanding of how to build a sustainable initiative from its very first idea. As will be evident from the acknowledgements, the sustainability of the ELSA project owes much, and relies much, on the commitment of many people. Implicitly, it celebrates what can be achieved through collaboration. Sheila has managed to infect many people, including me, with her enthusiasm for ELSAs and, of course, this is reciprocated. The enthusiasm of ELSAs has influenced the content of the training and the development of the role, quite apart from an ELSA's ability to infect the children and young people with whom they work with a sense of hope and wellbeing.

Enthusiastic collaboration is not the only thing that has sustained the programme. From the outset it relies upon the content of this manual: a rigorous training programme and a robust framework to ensure implementation. This framework includes the unqualified support of headteachers and an ELSA's line manager, a sound supervision process and other opportunities for continuing professional development. When I was training to be an educational psychologist, 'The Myth of the Hero Innovator' (Georgiades and Phillimore, 1975) was a much quoted and influential article. It seems to me that this article is as relevant today as when it was written, in the mid-seventies, and certainly relevant when thinking about the ELSA programme.

In essence, the article says that it is not enough to rely upon training alone to change how things get done. The authors draw attention to something we might all recognise. As a 'hero innovator' we can 'get eaten for breakfast' by disinterested colleagues and, particularly, line managers, when we return to our place of work, full of the bright ideas and skills that a training course introduced us to. The authors go on to suggest that 'cultivating the host culture' is crucial if staff training is going to be beneficial. This means, amongst other things, gaining management permission, support and encouragement for an initiative, developing a team approach where people can support each other to carry out the initiative, and working with those who favour the initiative rather than battling against those who oppose it.

At the beginning of the year, I found much to complement this when I heard Stephen Scott speak at a conference. Amongst other things he is the director of research for the National Academy of Parenting Practitioners hosted by King's College London. In talking about parenting programmes, he stressed, first, the importance of faithfully following a programme and second, and as might be expected, the skill of the professional delivering the programme does make a difference. For instance, in describing the Primary Age Learning Study, he drew attention to the observation that in measuring improvements to 'child aggression', the least skilful practitioners made things worse. The more skilful the professional, the greater was the improvement in this aspect of a child's behaviour.

In other words, we should not underestimate any of the elements that comprise the ELSA training programme and this manual. The product that you have in your hand has taken much time and patience to develop, and has benefited from careful evaluation. As a senior manager or School Improvement Partner in a Local Authority, as a headteacher or senior school manager you can be confident that it will enhance the mission of the school; as an ELSA you will experience enhanced job satisfaction; as an educational psychologist you will experience enhanced collaborative working with colleagues in schools. Above all, though, as a child or young person in a school with an ELSA, you will experience enhanced wellbeing. So, be faithful to it – and the ELSA programme will be faithful to you.

Dr Phil Stringer

County Services Manager/Principal Educational Psychologist

Part One

Project Planning

Chapter 1: Project Description

What is ELSA?

How do ELSAs Support Children and Young People?

Could a School have More than One ELSA?

Does ELSA Intervention Really Make a Difference?

Chapter 1: Project Description

What is an ELSA?

The Emotional Literacy Support Assistant (ELSA) project is an initiative of Hampshire Educational Psychology Service designed to build the capacity of schools to support the emotional needs of their pupils from within their own resources. It recognises that children learn better and are happier in school if their emotional needs are also addressed.

Since the introduction of a national curriculum, the educational focus in the United Kingdom has been principally on raising academic attainment in schools. Teacher training focuses almost exclusively on the national curriculum at the expense of a holistic view of child development. There has, however, been a growing appreciation by Government over recent years that to raise standards it is not sufficient to focus solely upon curriculum content and delivery. Schools should be concerned with the all round development of children and young people, as shown by the introduction of the Children Act 2004 (Every Child Matters) and the development of the Social and Emotional Aspects of Learning (SEAL) materials in primary and then secondary phases of education.

We know that the ability to learn is adversely affected by emotional and psychological difficulties. When emotional and cognitive energy is focused upon these things there is reduced capacity to concentrate on academic development and learning new skills. There will always be children and young people in our schools facing life challenges that detract from their ability to engage with learning. If we give them a chance to think about these difficulties within the context of a safe and supportive relationship, we can help them increase their resilience. By encouraging better recognition and self-management of emotional states they will become better able to access the educational opportunities presented to them.

All children should be nurtured in accordance with their individual needs. Just as with learning, some will require greater support to increase their emotional literacy than others. This may be able to take place within a small group or individually. The ELSA initiative was developed to provide that additional level of attention and care that will enable children with temporary or long-term emotional needs to feel better about themselves and about their time in school. Its aim is to equip school support staff to identify needs and intervene effectively to help create change for the pupils with whom they work. It is an initiative developed and supported by educational psychologists, who apply psychological knowledge of children's social and emotional development to particular areas of need and to specific casework. By working in this way, educational psychologists are able to indirectly support very many more young people than they could ever hope to do through direct involvement.

Hampshire ELSAs are Learning Support Assistants who have received five days additional training from educational psychologists on aspects of emotional literacy including emotional awareness, self-esteem, anger management, social and friendship skills. ELSAs are expected to be good listeners, help youngsters develop relationships of trust with them and assist them to increase their emotional literacy. The ELSAs receive supervision from educational psychologists once every half term in a local group of either primary or secondary ELSAs. They may also receive some additional individual support from the link psychologist for their school, as required.

How do ELSAs Support Children and Young People?

ELSAs are trained to plan and deliver programmes of support to pupils in their school who are experiencing temporary or longer term additional emotional needs. Programmes would normally last between half to one term, and occasionally a little longer. The majority of ELSA support is expected to be delivered on an individual basis, but sometimes some small group work will be appropriate, especially in the areas of social and friendship skills. Children may, for example, receive support to recognise and manage their emotions, raise their self-esteem, improve peer relationships, recover from significant loss or bereavement, and resolve conflict effectively.

ELSAs receive what is commonly referred to as clinical supervision from educational psychologists but are line managed from within their own schools. This is often the responsibility of the SENCO. Part of the line manager's role is to assist in the identification and prioritisation of pupils who would benefit from support. This is achieved in consultation with class teachers, form tutors, heads of year and the ELSAs themselves. Because they often also work in other contexts within the school, the ELSAs may also be able to identify appropriate candidates for intervention. The line manager may need to manage a waiting list for ELSA involvement.

In discussion with other staff in school the priorities for an individual pupil will be identified. These will inform the setting of aims for the programme, which are akin to individual education plan targets. With these in mind the ELSA plans support sessions to facilitate the young person in developing new skills and coping strategies that allow them to manage social and emotional demands more effectively. Each session would have its own objective that builds towards the longer term aims. Without clearly defined longer term aims it will be difficult for an ELSA to determine when a programme has run its course and sessions may be brought to a close.

Rather than using an ELSA as part of a pupil's permanent support structure, it is better to see her intervention as time-limited to assist the development of specific skills. Once new skills are acquired, time should be allowed for consolidation and generalisation. Further intervention towards additional aims could be considered at a later date if desired. Because the ELSA is part of the permanent staff within school, some informal contact may be maintained for a time to enable graduated withdrawal of support for those pupils who may need this. In some cases it may take the form of looking in on a pupil regularly for a few minutes, while for other pupils occasional review sessions may be more appropriate.

It must be appreciated by all concerned that change cannot necessarily be achieved rapidly and is dependent upon the context and complexity of the presenting issues. The training and development of ELSAs is an on-going process, so their own levels of experience and confidence should be taken into account when selecting pupils for support. Wisdom is required to recognise when issues are beyond the level of expertise that could reasonably be expected of an ELSA. The supervising psychologist or the school's own link psychologist would be able to offer advice on suitability or nature of ELSA involvement in complex cases.

Could a School have More than One ELSA?

There are many schools in Hampshire that have more than one ELSA. Indeed it was suggested from the outset that, in view of their size and organisational complexity, secondary schools would benefit from identifying two people for training. There is however a consequence upon the educational psychology service of allowing schools to train additional personnel, namely larger or an increased number of supervision groups. This places an increased pressure upon the educational psychology service. As the project grew it was decided in Hampshire to specify a limit on how many ELSAs a school could have – two for primary schools and three for secondary schools. The schools are, after all, in a position to increase the amount of time allocated to each ELSA for their work, as many have done.

If additional ELSAs are trained it is important to establish the principle that they are all allocated at least the minimum specified time for the role. Sometimes schools have sought to have more staff trained because of the value they place on the training and the desire for it to be accessed by learning support assistants in general. However they would not then wish to release all those trained for the supervision sessions each half term, or would not allocate sufficient time for those trained to properly fulfil an ELSA role.

There are nevertheless some distinct advantages to having at least two ELSAs within a school:

- If one is absent for a period of time on sickness or maternity leave the school is not left without this valuable support upon which they come to depend.

- If an ELSA leaves the school (some, for example, have gone on to train as teachers, moved from the area or retired) there is still some available support for pupils until another person can be trained.

- The ELSAs are easily able to provide each other with peer support, discussing intervention programmes, sharing ideas and problem-solving difficulties.

Does an ELSA Intervention Really Make a Difference?

In Hampshire there has been consistent positive feedback from schools that the introduction of ELSAs has made a significant positive impact on the emotional wellbeing of children and young people. Evaluation has been carried out in a variety of ways yielding both qualitative and quantitative evidence of its effectiveness. The results of evaluation studies are available from Hampshire Educational Psychology Service upon request, but reproduced below are a few examples of successful outcomes that have been reported:

- An ELSA worked with a Year 2 child whose parents had separated. The child had found this difficult to comprehend. He regularly spent time with both parents after school and during weekends. The child was angry and unsure about what his parents expected of him. The ELSA and pupil played therapeutic games and made a personal diary. In this way the boy was able to communicate his feelings of loss, anger and confusion. After several weeks he shared his diary with his parents. They were surprised by his emotional awareness. The child now regularly completes a feelings diary, opening up communication between himself and his parents.

- An ELSA worked with a boy in Year 4 who had both friendship and anger issues. He decided for himself he would like to work on his anger management as he thought his temper was one of the main reasons other children did not like him. The ELSA used ideas from 'A Volcano in my Tummy' (Whitehouse and Pudney, 1996) and solution focused brief therapy. The boy was committed to the work and ideas discussed. His manner (body language, self-confidence and smile) changed and was noticed by staff. His parents were pleased with his progress but, more importantly, he feels different about himself. He manages friendships and his anger much better, and is able to put calming strategies into practice.

- A secondary ELSA worked for over a year with an upper school pupil who was not attending regularly. She met with her every two weeks in order to discuss her lack of self-esteem and other problems she was facing. The girl would also seek her out at other times when she was not coping. Over a period of time her attendance increased dramatically. On her last day at school she thanked the ELSA for her support and asked to keep in touch by e-mail. She achieved excellent GCSE results.

Chapter 2: Planning the Introduction of the ELSA Project Within a Local Authority

Introduction

Who to Involve

Alternative Models for Setting up an ELSA Project:

Small-scale Pilot Project

Whole Local Authority Approach

Centrally Funded and Managed ELSA Service

Communication Strategy

PowerPoint Presentation – The ELSA Project (slides and notes)

Supporting Documents:

1. The ELSA Project: A Summary of the Project

Chapter 2: Planning the Introduction of the ELSA Project Within a Local Authority

Introduction

There are currently many hundreds of trained ELSAs working within Hampshire with the support of educational psychologists. The wish is to have ELSAs in every mainstream primary and secondary school within the county, as well as in special schools for pupils with behavioural, emotional and social or moderate learning difficulties. (Emotional literacy support is needed also for pupils with severe and complex learning difficulties, but would require a modified training course from the one presented here. Such support would be equally desirable in pre-school settings and would again require a differentiated training course.)

The initiative has already been successfully introduced elsewhere. Northumberland is one of the local authorities that have shown a strong commitment to this approach since it was first introduced there by a former Hampshire educational psychologist, Gillian Shotton, co-author of the handbook written to complement ELSA training (Shotton and Burton, 2008).

Who to Involve

As already indicated, in Hampshire this work rests within the domain of the educational psychology service. Educational psychologists have extensive training in children's emotional and social development and the psychology of learning. The training modules are founded on psychological knowledge and successful ELSA practice relies on the application of psychological understanding of learning and behaviour. If we accept that all behaviour has meaning, then seeking to uncover that meaning is crucial to helping pupils to develop more adaptive responses and coping strategies. It is our experience that ELSAs become involved in some complex casework which requires much more than the application of behavioural management strategies. While there may be other professionals within a local authority who could potentially contribute to the delivery of training, we in Hampshire would consider it vital that local authority psychologists are centrally involved in managing this work, especially in the provision of clinical supervision.

Alternative Models for Setting up an ELSA Project

Small-scale Pilot Project

The work in Hampshire initially began as a small-scale pilot project involving fourteen primary schools in one locality. Schools were invited to designate one learning support assistant to train for this work. The training days were delivered over a time span of approximately one term, with the trainee ELSAs gradually undertaking casework. The benefits of having a member of staff able to offer emotional literacy support to individual children quickly became apparent to headteachers and there was no difficulty signing up many more schools across a wider area the following year.

Running a pilot project also afforded the opportunity to demonstrate the model to other educational psychologists and gain their support to extend the work. This support was vital, not just in enabling several training cohorts to run simultaneously but most importantly in ensuring an ongoing commitment to provide group supervision to the growing number of ELSAs. A cascade model of training was adopted by the educational psychology service. The project co-ordinator led the initial training cohort in each area assisted by other local psychologists, who then went on to train additional cohorts without the co-ordinator.

The preferred size of training cohort has been thirty to thirty-five trainees with two trainers leading each training day. If a number of different trainers are used, it is preferable for there to be a consistent lead trainer throughout for reasons of continuity.

Decisions should made on whether to finance the training and necessary support from the core budget or seek additional funding sources. The time for training and supervision is taken from core service time in Hampshire, where allocations of time are not made to individual schools but to community educational psychologists who then prioritise work across their area. The time devoted to the ELSA work is justified on the grounds of indirect support to a number of schools simultaneously – a very time-efficient way of working. In services that operate a time allocation to schools system, time for training and supervision should be deducted prior to allocation.

Whole Local Authority Approach

Now that the efficacy of such an initiative has been demonstrated through extensive evaluation studies, some local authorities are ready to adopt a full-scale commitment to this work across their area from the beginning. This requires an educational psychologist to co-ordinate the project with the involvement of as many other colleagues as necessary to support the training and subsequent supervision groups. It is essential to have the support of the whole educational psychology service from the outset since this work will form a significant and long-term part of psychologists' service delivery. A full-time psychologist may be required to lead two or three supervision groups, depending on the size of group they are comfortable to facilitate. Each group will meet every half term for about two hours.

Thought should be given to how quickly to roll out training across the local authority. It may be preferable to space this sufficiently to allow some headteachers to experience the benefits for their school and spread the word to other colleagues. At a local authority level a decision must be taken on whether to delegate an additional part of the special educational needs budget to schools to pay specifically for ELSA time within schools if there is not already substantial financial delegation. In Hampshire, schools fund ELSAs from their own staffing budgets since a major part of the SEN budget has been delegated for many years.

Centrally-funded and Managed ELSA Service

The first ELSA initiative was a centralised service hosted within Southampton Psychology Service. Five peripatetic ELSAs were recruited from learning support staff in schools then managed and supervised from within the service, initially by the author. They worked with pupils referred to them by educational psychologists. While this is a workable model within a small unitary local authority it would be difficult to manage within a larger authority, not least because of the numbers needed and the travel distances involved.

Even within Southampton the ELSA work now follows a school-based model as an increasing number of schools saw the value of the approach and felt the need to dedicate their own learning support assistants to this work. Schools nominated their own staff to this role without any background training, although a training course has subsequently been created by the psychology service. Although there are now large professional support groups available to ELSAs in the city, there are as yet no clinical supervision groups to support ELSAs in their casework. This can leave them without access to appropriate support and represents a risk both to their own wellbeing and that of the pupils they work with.

One of the disadvantages of this model is that at the end of an intervention programme the pupil loses contact with the ELSA who ceases to visit them. It relies on others within school taking over support without necessarily having the desirable background knowledge, although this can be offset by adequate liaison prior to ending the involvement.

Dependant upon budgetary organisation, it could be feasible within a smaller authority to centrally fund and manage a large number of school-based ELSAs, but this would imply less control by school managers on how an ELSA in their school is deployed.

Communication Strategy

Whatever model is adopted, the ELSA initiative relies on a long-term partnership between the educational psychology service and schools. Supervision should be a permanent provision, not time-limited. Training should also continue as, even when the initiative is fully established, there will be a requirement to train additional ELSAs to replace those who move on from this role. Schools should allocate time, space and resources to the work on a long-term basis. Before embarking on the ELSA project it is essential that schools and the psychology service understand the rationale behind the initiative, the benefits to be gained and the continuing commitment required.

There will be a variety of ways to advertise the initiative within the local authority that might include the following:

- Word of mouth via educational psychologists.
- Letter to headteachers.
- Presentation to headteachers' conference.
- Broadsheet style newsletter comprising information provided within The ELSA Trainers' Manual and local project plans.

Before commencing any cohort of training, it is advisable to hold a launch meeting in advance for headteachers and SENCOs. A powerpointPowerPoint presentation entitled 'The ELSA Project' is provided for this purpose. A handout entitled 'The ELSA Project' provides a summary of the project and is found at the end of the chapter.

Once the project has begun to run in an area, it soon picks up a momentum of its own as other schools hear of it and begin to enquire about accessing training. It is useful to invite to a launch meeting a headteacher from a school that already has an ELSA, as other headteachers are able to hear direct from a colleague about its benefits.

Published evidence of its popularity and effectiveness is available in a journal article (Burton, S. 2008).

Slides 1-12

The ELSA Project

The ELSA Project

The ELSA Training Manual
Sheila Burton

Facilitator Notes for Slide 1

The facilitator will need the ELSA Project handout for this session.

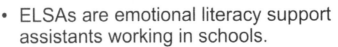

What is ELSA?

- ELSAs are emotional literacy support assistants working in schools.
- ELSAs help children recognise, understand and manage emotions to increase success.
- ELSAs plan and deliver individual (and small group) support programmes.
- ELSAs receive training and supervision from educational psychologists.

Facilitator Notes for Slide 2

The ELSA project is an initiative designed to help schools meet the needs of emotionally vulnerable pupils from within their own resources.

Children learn better and are happier in school if their emotional needs are met. When children's emotional and cognitive energy is focused on their personal and interpersonal difficulties, their capacity to concentrate on learning new information and skills is reduced.

ELSAs plan and deliver programmes of support to children identified within school as likely to benefit from additional help to increase their emotional literacy. Programmes would normally last between half to one term, and occasionally a little longer.

Children may, for example, receive support to recognise and manage their emotions, raise their self-esteem, improve peer relationships, recover from significant loss or bereavement, and resolve conflict effectively.

Most of the support is individual and builds on the relationship of trust that is developed between pupil and ELSA. Some skills will be enhanced through small group work, particularly social and friendship skills (although some children will need individual support first).

It is an initiative developed and supported by educational psychologists, who apply psychological knowledge of children's social and emotional development to particular areas of need and to specific casework.

The training has been developed by educational psychologists and ELSAs are provided with regular supervision to develop their understanding, skills and practice.

Origins

- Peripatetic ELSAs working for Psychology Service (Southampton).
- School-based ELSAs given training and supervision by Educational Psychology Service (Hampshire).
- School-based model adopted in other local authorities.

Facilitator Notes for Slide 3

As an educational psychologist working in Southampton, Sheila Burton originally developed this work with peripatetic ELSAs working within the psychology service. They went out to schools to work with primary school children identified by educational psychologists as needing additional emotional literacy support.

In Hampshire, Sheila developed an alternative model. Primary and secondary schools were invited to identify learning support assistants to be trained as ELSAs.

Educational psychologists provided five full days of training spread across one to two terms. This was followed up with approximately two hours of supervision in local groups every half term.

This was considered to be a more sustainable model and has since been adopted in various other local authorities.

Training Modules

- Emotional literacy in schools/raising emotional awareness.
- Self-esteem/active listening and communication skills.
- Anger management/working with puppets
- Social skills/autistic spectrum difficulties and social stories.
- Friendship skills/writing therapeutic stories.

Facilitator Notes for Slide 4

Day 1 provides an introduction to emotional literacy and the work of an ELSA. A good starting place for ELSA sessions is often to focus on the emotional awareness of a pupil – identifying a range of emotions and developing the vocabulary to express them.

Many children facing emotional challenges are likely to experience difficulties with self-esteem. On Day 2 this concept is broken down into specific aspects of self-esteem to help ELSAs plan appropriate support matched more closely to needs. There is also input on particular counselling skills that will assist communication between ELSAs and pupils.

The main focus of Day 3 is understanding anger and improving emotional self-regulation. There is also input on how to use puppets to enhance work with pupils of all ages.

Day 4 looks at social communication. Differences in the thinking style of autistic pupils are highlighted as these youngsters often benefit from social skills support. The principles of creating social stories are explained because these have been found to be very helpful in bringing about behavioural change.

Day 5 looks at the area of friendship. The skills needed to form and maintain friendships are considered. Finally, ELSAs are introduced to the technique of therapeutic story writing as a non-threatening way to help children reflect on their own behaviour and consider alternative strategies for meeting their needs.

Supervision

- Half-termly in cluster groups with link EP
- secondary ELSAs grouped together.
- 'Clinical' supervision (not managerial).
- Problem-solving approaches modelled.
- Peer group support – sharing ideas/resources.

Facilitator Notes for Slide 5

An essential part of the ELSA initiative is the ongoing support of educational psychologists to continue building the competence and confidence of ELSAs. Ideally this should take place in local cluster groups with the EP who works with those schools.

The reason for grouping secondary ELSAs together for supervision is that some different issues pertinent to adolescents will need to be considered. While universal training is perfectly appropriate, secondary ELSAs will need the opportunity to discuss specific needs with others likely to be dealing with similar issues.

There is a distinction between managerial and clinical supervision. ELSAs are line-managed within their own schools. Clinical supervision involves attention to the psychology behind needs and behaviour.

Within supervision groups useful problem-solving approaches can be modelled using the expertise of the supervising EP.

The groups also offer an opportunity to build supportive relationships between ELSAs, enabling the sharing of ideas and possibly some resources.

Essential Qualities for ELSAs

- Good rapport with challenging and emotionally vulnerable youngsters.
- Ability to work independently and creatively.
- Willing to plan and evaluate programmes of support.
- Desire to learn!

Facilitator Notes for Slide 6

It is vital for headteachers to think carefully about their choice of staff to train as ELSAs.

A prospective ELSA needs to have shown herself or himself to be able to build positive relationships with children who are not necessarily easy to get along with – both those who act out and those who are withdrawn.

That in itself is not enough. The initiative is predicated on the ability of ELSAs to think creatively about how to facilitate the development of new skills in the young people with whom they work. They must be able to work independently because they will be required to develop their own programmes of work, writing session plans and reflecting on outcomes.

Above all, an LSA wishing to become an ELSA will need to have the desire to learn, as there is a considerable amount of new learning involved in this role.

Psychology Service Commitment

- Deliver training to develop ELSA skills.
- Advise on planning programmes of support.
- Provide group supervision (and sometimes individual support).
- Advise on useful published resources.
- Assist in dissemination of 'home-grown' resources and ideas, and in problem-solving general ELSA issues.s

Facilitator Notes for Slide 7

Successful implementation of this initiative requires a firm commitment from the educational psychology service to continue training and support.

In addition to providing training and supervision, EPs will help ELSAs identify useful resources to support their work and help them with ideas for developing their own materials too.

They will also be able to recognise when an issue is beyond the reasonable scope of an ELSA and requires the involvement of a more specialist professional.

School Commitment

- Release ELSA for training and supervision sessions.
- Designate time for planning and delivery of ELSA support to pupils.
- Provide suitable space for ELSA work.
- Allocate funds to develop bank of resources over time.
- Maintain ELSA role within school.

Facilitator Notes for Slide 8

Equally important to successful outcomes is the commitment of the school in ensuring that:

- ELSAs are released for all training and supervision sessions
- they have ring-fenced time for adequate planning as well as the delivery of regular sessions to the children referred for support
- they have a suitable space (pleasant and semi-private) where they can work with pupils
- they have a budget which allows them to periodically purchase new resources (games, books, puppets) to develop their work
- finance is protected to maintain the ELSA role year on year.

Benefits to Pupils

- Pupils feel very supported by having 'special time' and being listened to.
- Pupils develop greater self-awareness.
- Pupils learn to talk about difficulties.
- Pupils develop coping strategies.
- Pupils interact more successfully with others.
- Pupils feel better about themselves.
- Pupils manage better in school.

Facilitator Notes for Slide 9

The impact of ELSA work in Hampshire has been thoroughly evaluated over time and has been published in national publications as well as internally.

These are some of the key benefits that have been shown:

- For some pupils it is the first time in their lives that any adult has given time to genuinely listen and understand how life is for them.

- ELSA intervention helps youngsters become more self-reflective and better at expressing their needs.

- They are helped to build more positive relationships, both with peers and adults, leading to improved self-esteem and greater success in terms of learning outcomes.

Benefits to School

- Access to prompt support for pupils in need.
- Positive changes in pupils with behavioural, emotional or social difficulties.
- Improved learning for target pupils and their peers.
- New skills/ideas cascaded to other staff.
- Increased confidence in managing 'problems' from within.

Facilitator Notes for Slide 10

There are clear benefits for the school as a whole:

- When emotional vulnerability is recognised there is a member of staff on hand who can offer support to pupils or advice to other staff.

- Behavioural difficulties have been shown to decrease in pupils who receive ELSA support for a period of time.

- This increases the learning not only of the pupil receiving input, but the knock-on effect of reduced disruption improves the learning environment for fellow classmates too.

- Other staff benefit from the new insights and skills that ELSAs bring to the school. Experience shows that ELSAs are often consulted by other staff about pupil concerns.

- Schools find themselves better able to manage pupil difficulties for themselves without having to wait for outside assistance.

Benefits to Psychology Service

- Indirect input to increased number of pupils.
- Continuity of support through regular supervision.
- Development of working relationship with ELSA through regular contact.
- Ability to contribute to school development
- Time and cost effective support to schools.

Facilitator Notes for Slide 11

The project requires significant EP time, which is justified by specific benefits for the educational psychology service too:

- By developing the skills and confidence of ELSAs, psychologists are able to impact a far greater number of children than they could ever do through direct casework involvement.

- Regular supervision allows them to deliver consistent support to schools over time. They develop good working relationships with ELSAs who are able to deliver the support an EP suggests to children with identified needs.

- Through the ELSA initiative the EP service is able to make a substantial contribution to school development. It has been shown to be an extremely time-effective and cost-effective way of deploying EP support.

Conclusion

The ELSA initiative is:

- a long-term partnership between the Educational Psychology Service and schools

- a tried and tested means of building capacity in schools

- an inexpensive way of providing quality support to vulnerable youngsters.

Facilitator Notes for Slide 12

In summary, this initiative involves a productive and long-term partnership between the Educational Psychology Service and local schools.

It has been shown over time to be effective in building capacity in schools to manage a variety of challenging pupil needs. EPs comment that some casework, which in the past might have come directly to them, is now dealt with effectively through ELSA intervention.

ELSAs are amongst the most inexpensive members of school staff yet are able to become highly skilled in meeting the needs of challenging and vulnerable pupils. Having an ELSA really makes a difference.

The ELSA Project – A Summary of the Project

The Emotional Literacy Support Assistant (ELSA) project is an initiative designed to build the capacity of schools to support the emotional needs of their pupils from within their own resources. It recognises that children learn better and are happier in school if their emotional needs are also addressed.

We know that the ability to learn is adversely affected by emotional and psychological difficulties. When emotional and cognitive energy is focused upon these things there is a reduced capacity to concentrate on academic development and learning new skills. There will always be children and young people in our schools facing life challenges that detract from their ability to engage with learning. If we give them a chance to think about these difficulties within the context of a safe and supportive relationship, we can help them increase their resilience. By encouraging better recognition and self-management of emotional states they will become better able to access the educational opportunities presented to them.

All children should be nurtured in accordance with their individual needs. Just as with learning, some will require greater support to increase their emotional literacy than others. The ELSA initiative was developed to provide that additional level of attention and care that will enable children with temporary or long-term emotional needs to feel better about themselves and about their time in school. Its aim is to equip school support staff to identify needs and intervene effectively to help create change for the pupils with whom they work. It is an initiative developed and supported by educational psychologists, who apply psychological knowledge of children's social and emotional development to particular areas of need and to specific casework. Through this project, educational psychologists are able to indirectly support very many more young people than they could ever do through direct involvement.

ELSAs are learning support assistants who have received five days additional training on aspects of emotional literacy including emotional awareness, self-esteem, anger management, social and friendship skills. They receive support from educational psychologists once every half term in a local primary or secondary supervision group. ELSAs are expected to be good listeners, build relationships of trust with young people and help them increase their emotional literacy. They plan and deliver programmes of individual (and sometimes small group) support that would normally last between half to one term, and occasionally a little longer. Children may, for example, receive support to recognise and manage their emotions, raise their self-esteem, improve peer relationships, recover from significant loss or bereavement, and resolve conflict effectively.

Chapter 2

Chapter 3: Planning Training

Identifying a Project Leader

Administrative Support

Contract with Schools

Selection of ELSAs

Certification of ELSAs

Supporting Documents:

1. ELSA Administration Protocol (sample) – what to do and when

2. ELSA Guidance for Schools – essential operational information

3. ELSA Training Contract – an agreement between schools and EP Service

4. ELSA Person Specification and Job Description – to guide ELSA selection

5. ELSA Certificate (sample)

.

Chapter 3: Planning Training

Identifying a Project Leader

ELSA is a long-term initiative that will grow over a period of time. It is therefore important to identify a committed project leader who will co-ordinate the planning and delivery of the project. The project leaders should be intimately involved with the project operationally to deal with issues as they arise, not simply managing it at a distance. They will be called upon to make decisions that would be hard to make without direct operational experience. This role is best undertaken by an educational psychologist but does not need to be a manager within the service.

The project leader will need to:

- Have an understanding of the principles behind this initiative (by reading The ELSA Trainers' Manual, the supporting text *Emotional Wellbeing: An Introductory Handbook* and the article referred to in the section on communication strategy).

- Liaise with all those involved in setting up the project to plan an implementation strategy.

- Agree a time-scale for implementation.

- Identify an administrative co-ordinator (see next section) with whom they will work closely to oversee the administrative requirements of the project.

- Oversee communication with schools (how, when, and so on).

- Be a point of contact for schools inquiring about the project.

- Run the launch meeting – presenting, responding to questions.

- Plan delivery of training in conjunction with other trainers.

- Oversee the organisation of supervision groups (how many, where, identification of supervisors and allocation of ELSAs to groups).

- Ensure support for the educational psychologist supervisors (liaison over process and content of supervision, reflection on issues brought to supervision by ELSAs).

- Be a confident and effective problem-solver!

Administrative Support

There will inevitably be a significant amount of administration involved in running the ELSA project and the project leader will need support from a confident administrator who will take responsibility for much of the practical organisation. The protocol written by the administrative lead in Hampshire is included at the end of the chapter as an example of what might be involved.

Contract with Schools

To implement the ELSA project requires a significant commitment of staffing resource by the local authority, particularly educational psychology time. It is a long-term partnership with schools to provide a service that will enhance their capacity to meet the needs of a wide range of emotionally vulnerable pupils. For the project to operate successfully there must be a commitment from participating schools to do all that is necessary to ensure ELSAs are enabled to carry out their responsibilities effectively. A sample contract is included at the end of this section and it is strongly recommended that headteachers be asked to sign this before a member of their staff is accepted for training.

One of the key factors is protecting adequate time for the role. It is recommended that a minimum of a day a week be allowed (although in very small schools of less than a hundred pupils half a day may be adequate). With any less time than this an ELSA will not have reasonable opportunity to put into practice the knowledge and skills developed through training. This creates frustration for the ELSA herself and for the local authority staff investing time and energy into the project.

An ELSA will be seriously hampered in his role if the school does not allocate an adequate budget for resources. One of the reasons that pupils engage so well with this support is that the sessions are very different from subject lessons. ELSA sessions should never become over-dependant upon activity pages. They should be highly interactive and learning is most effective if mediated through games and other practical activities. There is a fantastic range of published resources that will engage pupils in personal reflection and problem-solving. These are inevitably costly, but are generally durable and likely to be used many times over with successive clients. As with any curriculum subject it is essential for an ELSA to be able to build up a wide and varied collection of resources over time to support his work and enable him to remain innovative in his planning.

Every ELSA will need a copy of Emotional Wellbeing: An introductory handbook. This was specifically written as a text to support ELSA training, covering each area of focus within the course. During training the ELSAs will be expected to read related chapters following each day's input. The publication is available online from the site below: http://www.teachingexpertise.com/publications/emotional-wellbeing-an-introductory-handbook-2389. A PDF file is available for the trainer's use only on the CD-ROM provided with this publication.

The ELSA's line manager should help other staff understand the nature of the intervention offered and the rationale behind it. This will avoid difficulties arising such as reluctance to release pupils from part of the curriculum, reluctance to release the ELSA from classroom responsibilities as a learning support assistant in order to fulfill the responsibilities of the ELSA role, or the misperception that giving ELSA support to a challenging pupil is rewarding bad behaviour.

In response to some of the difficulties commonly reported by ELSAs in supervision sessions, a guidance document entitled ELSA Guidance for Schools was written for school managers and is included at the end of the chapter, along with a model contract to be signed by headteachers.

Selection of ELSAs

Not all learning support assistants will be suited to the role of ELSA. It is vital to identify the best people for the job. Simply asking who within school is interested is not a responsible way of responding to this training opportunity.

The majority of ELSAs report high levels of job satisfaction. They appreciate the value placed on their role by colleagues within school, and gain great satisfaction from seeing the difference their involvement makes on the children with whom they work. It is certainly a demanding role and as their colleagues become aware of their growing expertise, ELSAs find themselves being asked to take on increasingly complex casework.

As well as being approachable and nurturing, ELSAs need to be self-motivated and resilient. Not all their clients are equally responsive or appreciative of the support provided. There will be times for any ELSA when he doubts his own ability, which underlies yet again the importance of supervision from skilled professionals. To assist headteachers in selecting appropriately skilled support staff for this role, a person specification and job description is provided at the end of the chapter.

Certification of ELSAs

In Hampshire the ELSA training has not at this point been externally accredited, although this has been pursued elsewhere. Northumberland has negotiated accreditation with the Open College Network. The level to which the training could be accredited would depend on the assignment requirements of ELSAs. If this option were pursued, it would be unwise to make it a condition of training. There are many extremely good ELSA practitioners who would find the requirement of marked assignments an unwelcome pressure and a discouragement to participation in the project. However, if participants are keen to keep a file for possible future accreditation of prior experiential learning, this can be encouraged.

As supervision is viewed as an essential component of the ELSA project, certificates are not awarded in Hampshire upon completion of the five initial training days. ELSAs are expected to attend a minimum of four supervision sessions before receiving a certificate so that there can be a level of confidence that the ELSA model of practice is being followed.

If an ELSA is absent for any part of the training, a note is made and a place offered on the next available cohort for the module that was missed. Each of the modules has been developed to reflect a key area of pupil intervention and it is therefore desirable that all ELSAs have the same preparatory input. Certification is delayed until all training and supervision requirements are fulfilled.

A sample certificate is included at the end of the chapter as a guide.

ELSA Administration Protocol (Sample)

Waiting List

Maintain a waiting list of schools wanting training (to include trainees who have previously missed an odd day and want to complete the course).
Where schools are applying to have an additional ELSA trained, check with respective link EPs that they are happy for those schools to have additional ELSA training (that is, that they are using their existing ELSAs effectively).

When a Training Course is to be Run (Probably One Each Academic Year)

Set up a sub-folder on computer especially for that cohort, under the name of the Lead EP, and open a ring-binder for the same purpose.

Launch Meeting/Advertising the Training

The launch meeting is for headteachers/SENCOs of schools who haven't previously had an ELSA trained.
Consult Lead EP about date, venue, cost and so on of launch meeting – make appropriate booking and confirm in writing.
Book PowerPoint projector for launch meeting.
Consult Lead EP about dates, venue, cost and so on of actual training – make bookings – so that this information can be made known to schools right from the start.
Arrange refreshments (tea/coffee/biscuits), speakers ('successful' head, good ELSA).
Write to headteachers (copy to SENCO in separate envelope) inviting them to launch meeting and enclosing contract which gives details of dates/venue/cost of actual training, map of venue of launch meeting, person specification, and reply slip giving closing date (see sample set of papers attached):

- One letter to schools on waiting list who haven't previously had ELSA trained and inviting them to launch meeting.

- Different letter to schools on waiting list who have previously had ELSA trained (mention launch meeting, but they don't need to attend).

- A third letter to schools who have never had an ELSA trained, offering training and inviting to launch meeting.

Collate responses.
Prepare register for launch meeting.

Keep link EPs informed if schools raise any specific comments in their replies (for example, those who do not wish to take part in ELSA training).
After launch meeting, write to thank speakers as appropriate (for example, headteacher, experienced ELSA).

Chapter 3

Training Course

Collect signed contracts from schools and create/maintain a list. Chase any schools who had expressed an interest in training but who didn't return contract by closing date.

Book PowerPoint projector for each day of training.

Send parked journals to schools for cost of training.

Arrange for ELSA folders to be printed.

Prepare registers (one for each of the five days), not forgetting to add name of anyone who is catching up on an individual day/s from previous a course.

Write to the trainee ELSAs confirming their place, dates and time of training, and enclosing map of venue, plus copy of letter for headteacher/SENCO; also send list of trainees so that transport can be combined where possible.

On Day 1 or 2, give trainees a copy of their respective school's signed contract.

Contact trainees who are catching up on the odd day that they have missed previously and give them the appropriate date/s and venue; send written confirmation.

Lead EP will enlist EPs to support the training.

Copy trainees' letter and so on to the EPs who are tutoring on the training so they have map and so on.

Consider asking experienced ELSA to give a talk on Day 5.

Arrange refreshments for the five days' training when number known; need to check how many EPs/trainers for each day, as well as trainees.

Reconfirm with venue/catering nearer the time.

Check which activity packs are required for each day's training and ensure there are sufficient for the number on the course.

Warn EPs delivering training to allow time/space for collection of folders from the office.

At the training on Day 1, check spelling of name of each trainee so that the name recorded on our master list is correct (especially for certificate).

To remind headteachers/SENCOs of their ELSA commitment, either:

- arrange headteachers/SENCOs of schools who are having ELSAs trained to attend at the end of Day 5 of the training (and invite ELSAs to stay on for that meeting too)

- write to headteachers/SENCOs after Day 5 to remind them of their commitment.

At the venue, put up signs to ask trainees to:

- sign the register

- leave their badges in a box at the end of the day for next time

- hand in their evaluation forms (put a tray out for this).

Finance

- With the Lead EP, calculate the cost of the training and set a fee for each trainee.
- When contracts received from schools, charge the schools via SAP (some schools may send two trainees, so charge accordingly).
- Keep note of income and expenditure in the form of a balance sheet.
- Pay invoices on receipt (venue, catering and so on).
- Produce a final balance sheet on completion of training.

Evaluation of Training

A comments form is included in the course materials for Days 1-4. A formal evaluation form is included for Day 5. All forms should be collected in at the end of each day and brought in to the office. Collate the ratings; ensure that tutors have read the written comments. Record the ratings and keep in working file, and summarise improvement suggestions for Lead EP. Ensure action taken on any significant comment.

Supervision Venues

Make a list of schools which offer venue for supervision sessions (there's provision for this on the contract) and email the resultant list to EPs.

Master List of ELSAs and Cohorts

Maintain the ELSA database in Excel.
Update list of cohorts trained.
At the end of each academic year, remind all EPs to let the co-ordinator know the latest re any changes to ELSAs (some will have left, some will have changed school, some will have changed their names, some need certificates) and cohorts.
Be prepared to supply project leader with statistics of yearly training numbers and so on.

ELSA Certificates

ELSA certificates are awarded to trainees when they have attended all five days' training, have subsequently attended at least four supervision sessions with EPs, and are doing the work effectively in their school. It is up to the co-ordinator to arrange a system for recording attendance and issuing the certificates.
- Check the date is appropriate.
- Print on white card.
- Project leader will sign the certificate.
- The certificate should be laminated.
- Send with a compliments slip in a board-backed envelope to the school.

Reminder: Update database when certificates are awarded.

Elaine Howells, Hampshire Educational Psychology Service.

ELSA Guidance for Schools

ELSA is a proactive, not reactive intervention. Although ELSAs, because of their personal qualities and skills, may be well equipped to deal with the aftermath of conflict incidents, such involvement is outside the specific parameters of their ELSA role and would require additional time. The role itself involves the development of programmes of support that are delivered over a period of time (usually at least six weeks and sometimes significantly longer) which are aimed at reducing future difficulties.

Selection of Pupils for ELSA Intervention

ELSAs receive what is commonly referred to as clinical supervision from educational psychologists but are line managed from within their own schools. This is often the responsibility of the SENCO. Part of the line manager's role is to assist in the identification and prioritisation of pupils who would benefit from support. This is achieved in consultation with class teachers, form tutors, heads of year and the ELSAs themselves. Because they often also work in other contexts within the school, the ELSAs may also be able to identify appropriate candidates for ELSA intervention. The line manager may need to manage a waiting list for their involvement.

It should be appreciated by all concerned that change cannot necessarily be achieved rapidly and is dependent upon the context and complexity of the presenting issues. The training and development of ELSAs is an on-going process, so their own levels of experience and confidence should be taken into account when selecting pupils for support. Wisdom is required to recognise when issues are beyond the level of expertise that could reasonably be expected of an ELSA. The supervising psychologist or the educational psychologist who normally works with the school would be able to offer advice on suitability or nature of ELSA involvement in complex cases.

Effective Line Management

Although ELSAs are selected partly on their ability to show initiative and be self-managing of their work, good line management greatly enhances the effectiveness of their role. In addition to supporting the selection of pupils for intervention there are other key responsibilities for the line manager:

Time – ensuring the ELSA has adequate time to plan and deliver programmes and to reflect upon sessions.

Workspace – making available appropriate space which affords a comfortable environment and degree of privacy for pupils.

Agreeing targets – helping to define measurable and achievable targets for the programme which will facilitate decisions about duration of support, that is, when it can be drawn to a close.

Progress review – periodically reviewing session plans and discussing pupil progress and needs.

Liaison – assisting liaison and effective collaboration with other staff and parents, so that appropriate information is shared and new pupil skills are generalised into the wider contexts of home and school.

Protecting confidentiality – ensuring pupils' rights to an appropriate level of confidentiality with the ELSA and ensuring the ELSA is aware of safeguarding issues and child protection procedures.

Provision of resources – allocating a budget that enables the ELSA to purchase resources to assist his/her work.

Appraisal – reviewing ELSA performance, agreeing targets for personal professional development and identifying any additional support or training needed.

Duration of ELSA Involvement

It would normally be expected for a programme to last at least half a term and often a little longer. However it should be exceptional for a programme of intervention to last beyond one and a half terms. This tends to occur if targets have not been clearly defined. It is better to plan for multiple shorter term programmes with changing focus than for continuous long-term involvement which risks creating dependency. Once a pupil has been introduced to new skills he will need time to consolidate and generalise those skills. Ideally he will have had some input into targets so that he takes some personal ownership of his own progress. Once a programme of support reaches a natural conclusion support does not have to cease completely. The ELSA may arrange less frequent review opportunities or maintain regular brief contact which some pupils would find reassuring.

Session Frequency and Duration

The length of sessions will depend upon the age and concentration span of pupils. Generally they are likely to be from half an hour up to a maximum of one hour in a secondary school. In this case it would be wise to allow ten minutes for a self-chosen independent activity at the end of the session to allow the ELSA to complete reflective notes or prepare for her next session. In primary schools it is usually easier to return a pupil to class mid-lesson. Most pupils will receive weekly input but occasionally more frequent shorter sessions may be appropriate, particularly with the youngest children. Like good lessons, a good ELSA session should involve a variety of activities and be delivered with pace. This can only be achieved with adequate planning. ELSAs are given advice on how to write brief session plans which should include a short reflection afterwards of how the session went. These documents are kept as an intervention record and ensure accountability within school.

Deciding Between Individual and Group Work

On the face of it line managers may consider group work to be a more economic use of ELSA time. However the underlying premise of this work is that most of it should be on an individual basis. The needs of children requiring this kind of support are likely in the main to be quite specific and individual, even when working within the same area of focus. Evaluation has shown that one of the most significant success factors is the development of a relationship of trust between an ELSA and pupil that allows the young person to open up in a way that they may never have done to anyone else. For some children, working with an ELSA is their first experience of anyone ever really giving them time to talk and listening to their thoughts and feelings with genuine interest. The addition of other children inevitably changes the dynamic and may be a constraining factor. However, there may be good reason for incorporating some group work, especially when working on social and friendship skills. Yet even in these areas it may be necessary in some cases to begin with individual work and subsequently to provide a group context in which to practise new skills. Where group work is considered beneficial, a maximum size of not more than six pupils is advised. It is vital to give very careful consideration to the make-up of any group as the experience can easily be undermined by a negative dynamic.

Importance of Maintaining Consistency

Consistent support gives a young person an important message of being valued within the school community. The reliability of this support is vital. Anyone who has ever been a client in a counselling relationship knows the importance of appointments being honoured. When pupils are expecting to see their ELSA they are likely to have things they wish to share with her, and sometimes it requires a build up of courage for them to do so. If she is suddenly unavailable they may experience considerable disappointment. Cancellation of a session is sometimes unavoidable. If it is a planned cancellation because of a training or supervision commitment, the pupil should be warned in advance. If it is unplanned because of unexpected illness it is important to let pupils know at the beginning of the day so that disappointment is reduced. It is unacceptable for ELSAs to be routinely diverted from their ELSA work because of staffing shortages or other curricular needs. Schools are urged to safeguard time for this pastoral support work and not see it as a flexible commodity. Failure to do so will cause effectiveness of the provision to be reduced.

Sustaining the Role

A significant amount of training and supervision time is involved in developing a confident and competent ELSA. It is therefore in a school's best interests to sustain the role. It is both uneconomic and disruptive when there are frequent changes of personnel as new ELSAs require a significant amount of time to get up to speed with their new responsibilities. ELSAs feel valued and supported when their schools follow the guidelines above. When time for the work is protected, it is adequately resourced and they receive appropriate recognition for the work they do, ELSAs report high levels of job satisfaction.

Chapter 3

ELSA Training Contract

Commitment from the Facilitator

The facilitator will deliver five days' training (9.00am-3.30pm), spread across the autumn 2009 and spring term 2010. Training will take place at:

....

The following topics will be covered, on the under-mentioned dates:

(Date)	An Introduction to Emotional Literacy, Raising Emotional Awareness
	Self-esteem An Introduction to Active Listening and Communication Skills in Working with Children
	Anger Management
	Social Skills Training An Introduction to Autism
	Friendship Skills Therapeutic Stories

After completion of this training, group supervision will be provided half-termly to school clusters, normally by the link EP. Supervision sessions will last approximately two hours. ELSAs from secondary schools will be grouped together for supervision to ensure an appropriate professional peer group.

Commitment from School

The school will nominate one LSA (identified as having the necessary prerequisite skills to train as an ELSA, see attached) who will then be released for the five whole-day training sessions and for the half-termly supervision sessions. In some cases, two LSAs can be trained.

The school will also need to release each ELSA for at least the equivalent of one day per week to plan and deliver programmes of support to individual pupils nominated by the school. For very small schools (for example, 100 pupils or fewer) half a day may be sufficient. A member of the teaching staff should be nominated to line-manage the ELSA.

The school will have to allocate approximately £500 for the purchase of appropriate emotional literacy resources during the first year, which should include 'Emotional Wellbeing: an introductory handbook' by Gillian Shotton and Sheila Burton, published by 'Teach To Inspire' at £29. This handbook has been written specifically to accompany ELSA training. See website: www.teachingexpertise.com/teachtoinspire. A further budget allocation should be made each subsequent year to enable ELSAs to develop an appropriate bank of resources in response to needs.

A charge of (cost) per ELSA will be made and this will be charged before the course starts. To keep project costs to a minimum, participating schools will be asked to host supervision sessions.

Name of school: ....

We wish to participate in ELSA training, beginning October 2009, and agree to the terms of involvement outlined above. We agree to release each ELSA for every training day, plus twice-termly supervision sessions. We agree to allocate time each week, as specified, to ELSAs to fulfil their responsibilities.

Signed: ....

Date: ....

Designation: ....

Name/s of ELSA/s to be trained:

(a) ....

(b) ....

School SAP org unit number (to enable payment for training):

....

We would be able to provide a venue for one of the group supervision sessions: Yes/No

Please return to: (name and address of administrative officer) by courier or fax to (fax number) by (date).

Chapter 3

ELSA Person Specification and Job Description

Person Specification

The ideal potential ELSA:

- has a warm personality
- is able to stay calm under pressure
- demonstrates good interpersonal skills with children and adults
- is able to gain the confidence of children who are behaviourally challenging or socially withdrawn
- enjoys learning
- is able to work independently and show initiative
- has good time management and organisational skills
- is able to plan programmes of support that incorporate variety, interest and pace
- is able to keep succinct records of involvement.

Job Description

The role requires the ELSA to:

- attend training days and group supervision sessions led by the facilitator
- plan and deliver individualised programmes of support for children to develop their emotional literacy, including:
  - awareness of own and other people's emotions
  - development of an increased range of emotional vocabulary
  - management of stress, grief, anger and conflict
  - development of social interaction skills
  - development of the ability to initiate and maintain friendships
  - promotion of a realistic self-concept and good self-esteem
- plan and deliver programmes of support to small groups of children to develop social and friendship skills
- write succinct session plans and add subsequent evaluative comments
- liaise with teachers and other support assistants about the needs and progress of children receiving support
- share knowledge and ideas from training/supervision sessions with other school staff as appropriate
- meet regularly with line manager to review ELSA work
- work within own competencies and level of development, under the guidance of the line manager
- liaise with parents in line with school policy.

Example prepared by the Hampshire Educational Psychology Service.

The ELSA Project

This is to certify that

....

has been trained by

....

as an Emotional Literacy Support Assistant

Date ....

ELSAs attend five days' training in emotional literacy support;
plan and carry out emotional literacy work with pupils in school;
and attend half-termly group supervision sessions.

Signed ....

Chapter 4: Planning Supervision

Rationale for Supervision

Leading a Supervision Group

Supporting Documents:

1. Supervision of ELSAs (sample policy) – explanation for schools

Chapter 4: Planning Supervision

Rationale for Supervision

Ideally a supervision group would comprise ELSAs based in schools local to each other and be led by the educational psychologist who works with those schools, but this may not always be possible, particularly in the early stages of a project. The advantage is that the psychologist will be familiar with the contexts in which those ELSAs work and would be well placed to offer additional casework support on a school visit as appropriate. This enables continuity of advice. They would also have the potential to assist directly in problem-solving any operational difficulties within a school. If a different educational psychologist runs the group, there may be occasions when liaison with the psychologist for the school is important.

For ELSAs from secondary schools a different arrangement is recommended. There will be supervision issues specific to adolescents that make it desirable to group them together, with the obvious implication that they will be drawn from a larger geographical area and may not be with the educational psychologist for their school. Some of the pupil issues that have been raised in secondary supervision groups include alcohol and substance abuse, eating disorders, self-harming, inappropriate attachment to an ELSA, relationship fantasies about members of staff and under age sexual relationships between peers.

It is important for supervisors to be alert to needs that would require more specialist input than an ELSA could reasonably be expected to offer. This depends upon the complexity of the issues and individual pupil factors. It is not as simple as defining areas for involvement and areas where involvement is inappropriate. Take, for example, self-harming behaviour. An ELSA may be able to successfully support a young person who is experimenting with self-harm in imitation of other pupils. If however a young person engages in self-harming behaviour as a consequence of being seriously abused they are likely to require specialist professional intervention.

Supervision arrangements must be agreed by the final day of training so that ELSAs can be informed of the group to which they have been assigned, name of the group supervisor, time and date of first meeting and venue. At this time the rationale and importance of supervision must be explained.

A suggested guidance document which outlines the policy in Hampshire and is entitled Supervision of ELSAs is included at the end of the chapter as a useful summary for ELSAs and for their line managers in school.

Leading a Supervision Group

It is advised that the educational psychologist leading a supervision group complete an attendance register for each session. This allows any non-attendance to be monitored. Irregular attendance should be followed up with the school so that difficulties may be resolved. If, for example, a school has more than one ELSA and finds it difficult to release both simultaneously, one of them could be assigned to an alternative group that meets at a different time.

It is a matter of choice for the supervisor whether to make and circulate any notes of the meeting, to which they could also attach printed resources contributed by ELSAs. Some groups have appreciated this, but other supervisors may find that writing notes detracts from the supervision process. If notes are kept they should respect confidentiality and avoid recording personal information that could identify individual children. In either case, ELSAs should be encouraged to make their own notes of things relevant to their needs.

In any newly formed group participants need to get to know each other and develop trust. Within the supervision group there must be an understanding that information is shared in confidence and should be treated with respect by all. If any matter is raised that should be referred elsewhere by the supervisor, this should be with the knowledge of the ELSA concerned and confidentiality issues respected. ELSAs should also be made aware that supervisors themselves receive supervision. This is normal practice in any kind of therapeutic work.

Since supervision is a means of ensuring continuing professional development, supervisors need to be mindful of a balance of content that allows for extending knowledge, understanding and skills while developing the problem-solving skills of ELSAs themselves. There may be occasions when the session is used for some supplementary training in a specific area. This should not however be allowed to become the regular expectation of the group as it would take away from the ELSAs' responsibility to share together and reflect upon personal practice.

Supervision is an opportunity to introduce a group to a range of problem-solving approaches. The use of some formal processes can be a useful way of ensuring that all have a reasonable opportunity to participate in the process, thereby preventing domination of the session by one or two more vocal members of the group. It can also protect the supervisor from an expectation that they should provide all the answers and become the source of all knowledge for the group.

The supervision meetings provide opportunity for:

- supervisors to check on how ELSAs are developing in their role
- supervisees to share good practice as they reflect upon successful interventions
- shared problem-solving of any difficult issues
- exploration of different areas of pupil need
- the sharing of new resources
- aspects of training to be revisited
- additional training in areas of relevance.

When considering pupil behaviours, the supervising psychologist has an important role in helping ELSAs consider the communicative function of that behaviour. This is a time for generating hypotheses which the ELSA bringing the case can consider, looking for evidence that either supports or refutes the different hypotheses. This is a crucial process for maintaining a child-centred focus that separates the behaviour from the emotional responses of those dealing with it.

Finally, supervisors should remember that they do not need to be experts in all areas of pupil need that ELSAs bring to supervision. It is alright to say, 'I don't know.' This provides an opportunity for all members of the group to go away and find out more on any given topic.

Supervision of ELSAs

Example from the Hampshire Educational Psychology Service.

ELSA Recognition

In Hampshire, the title of ELSA is only recognised to legitimately apply to those who have undertaken the designated training with Hampshire Educational Psychology Service and continue to receive regular supervision from educational psychologists.

Who should Supervise ELSAs?

As ELSAs are employed directly by schools, they should receive management supervision from a nominated member of staff. This may be the SENCO or another manager within the school. The line manager is responsible for supporting ELSAs in their day-to-day work by ensuring that they have designated time for planning and delivery, a suitable space in which to work with children, and a budget for purchasing resources appropriate to their work. The line manager will also liaise with the ELSA about children in need of support, and help other staff to be aware of the role of the ELSA within school. It is the responsibility of the line manager to ensure that ELSAs are released from other responsibilities to attend training and supervision.

In addition, because of the nature of their work, ELSAs also need regular access to professional supervision with educational psychologists. EPs are responsible not only for initial training but also the ongoing professional development and support of ELSAs. The principal means of providing continuing support is through local supervision groups facilitated by EPs. These meet for two hours twice a term to:
- provide casework support through the application of psychological perspectives
- enable additional training in areas not covered in the initial five days
- disseminate information about useful resources
- give access to peer support
- facilitate shared problem-solving.

ELSAs are working with some of the most vulnerable and sometimes challenging young people in our schools. For their own safety and that of the young people they are supporting, it is essential that ELSAs continue to receive specialised professional support that enables them to reflect on the quality and appropriateness of the assistance they are offering. Schools should have due regard to the skills and competence of the ELSA and not be asking them to work beyond their competence. EPs may also advise further discussion with line manager when a young person's needs seem to be beyond the skills and competence of an ELSA and require more specialist support.

Chapter 4

In addition to group supervision twice a term, ELSAs are encouraged to seek individual consultation with the school's link EP if they are uncertain of how to proceed in a particular case or with respect to a specific issue that ought not to be left until the group next meets. Since ELSAs are known to be supporting youngsters with complex emotional needs, best practice is for link EPs to have some regular contact with ELSAs in the course of school visits.

What will Happen if an ELSA Does Not Attend Supervision?

Receiving a certificate of training is contingent upon ELSAs attending all five days of initial training and participating in four supervision sessions following completion of training. Once they have received their ELSA certificate, they are required to continue accessing regular supervision.

The EPs facilitating the groups are expected to keep a register of attendance. ELSA attendance is then recorded centrally to ensure that they are receiving adequate professional support. Inevitably there will be occasions when, for reasons beyond their control, an ELSA is unable to attend a group supervision session. In such circumstances, apologies should be sent to the facilitating EP. If non-attendance is noticed to be a regular occurrence, the link EP will be asked to make enquiries of the school and attempt to rectify the situation.

Where there is more than one ELSA in a school and releasing two or more people at the same time creates difficulties for the school, the EP service will be happy to allocate the ELSAs concerned to different groups.

If an ELSA chooses to discontinue attending supervision meetings or is prevented by the school from doing so, they will be assumed to be no longer functioning in an ELSA role and their name will be removed from the register of county approved ELSAs. They will no longer be eligible for places at further ELSA training events.

This is to ensure that ELSAs are given the necessary professional and ethical guidance to enable them to fulfill their responsibilities to children and young people to an appropriate standard. The educational psychology service recognises its responsibility in this area and consequently prioritises its support to ELSAs.

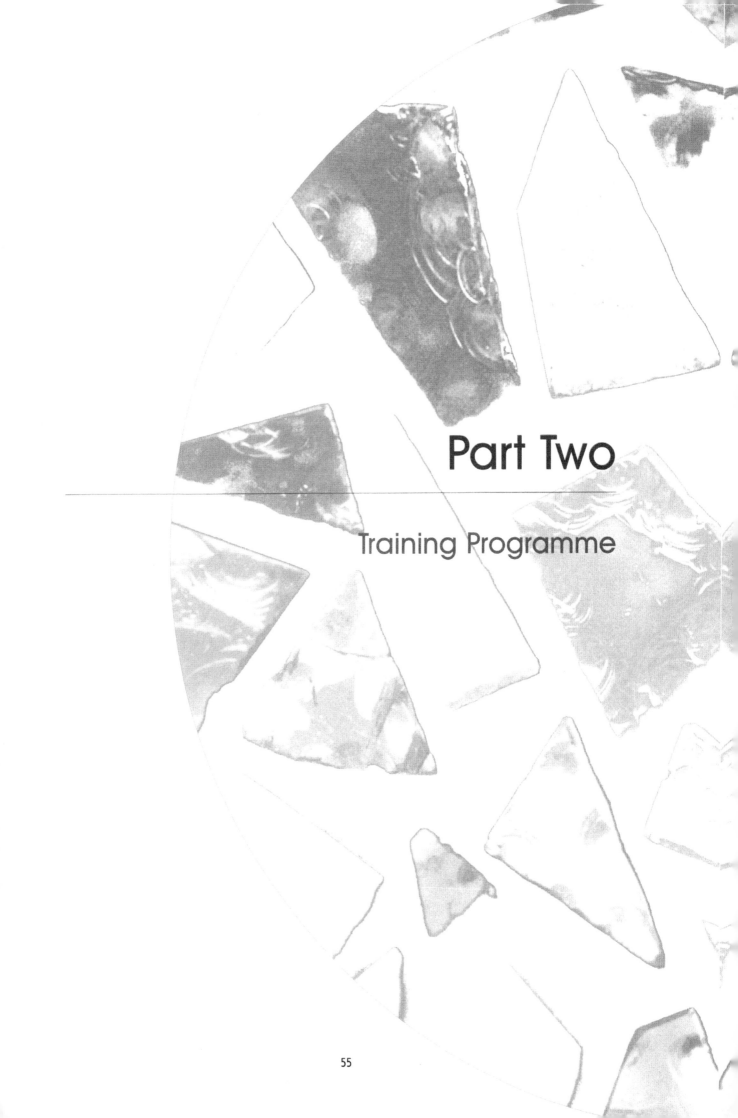

Part Two

Training Programme

Day 1

Content and Plan

PowerPoint Presentation – Emotional Literacy in Schools (slides and notes)

> Supporting Documents:
>
> > 1. Maslow's Hierarchy of Human Needs – handout (Linked to Slide 6)
> >
> > 2. Fenman EQ – Self-test – activity page (Linked to Slide 35)
> >
> > 3. Fenman EQ – Self-test Score Sheet – activity page (Linked to Slide 35)
> >
> > 4. Fenman Stop, Start, Continue – activity page (Linked to Slide 35)

PowerPoint Presentation – Raising Emotional Awareness (slides and notes)

> Supporting Documents:
>
> > 1. Emotional Expression – handout (Linked to Slide 5)
> >
> > 2. Feelings – suggested activities for ELSAs
> >
> > 3. Getting Started – guidance notes for ELSAs
> >
> > 4. ELSA Referral Form – for schools to refer pupils for ELSA support
> >
> > 5. Session Planning Guidelines for ELSAs
> >
> > 6. ELSA Session Plan – planning proforma for ELSAs
> >
> > 7. Letter to Parents/Carers (Sample) – to inform parents/carers of ELSA support
> >
> > 8. Information for Parents/Carers (Primary Sample) – to explain ELSA role

Day 1

Content and Plan

The focus of the day is on introducing the trainee ELSAs to the project, both to its rationale and how it works. At this stage they are likely to have very little idea of what is expected of them. By the end of this first day they should have an understanding of what is meant by emotional literacy and its impact on pupil success. They will be ready to at least begin planning a programme based on raising emotional awareness, and may even manage to start working with a pupil before the second training day.

The initial session is a welcome to the course and general introduction to the project. It is an opportunity to give the trainees a clearer idea about what they are training to do and how they will be supported in developing their new role.

This first presentation explains the concept of emotional literacy and how it impacts on the success of pupils in school. Self-reflection is encouraged since it is an underlying principle that emotional literacy cannot simply be taught. It should be modeled and facilitated. If we are to help young people recognise, understand and manage their emotions more effectively then we need to become increasingly skilled in emotional self-management.

The second presentation considers the need to develop children's ability to talk about their feelings, thereby reducing the need to display them through unhelpful behaviours.

But in order to talk about feelings, we must first recognise different emotional states and have the vocabulary to differentiate between them.

Some general principles are set out in the document entitled 'Getting Started' which should be explained and discussed with the trainees.

Time should be allowed for some initial planning in groups. It is therefore helpful from the outset of the course to encourage the trainees to sit with colleagues working in the same school phase (infant, junior, general primary or secondary). This will enable their discussions and group activities to be focused on pupils of an age they are familiar with.

There should be a short plenary session to check on how trainees are feeling at the end of this introductory day and to clarify expectations of what they will do before the next training day, including the follow-up reading. It would also be useful to give them a copy of the supporting document entitled ELSA Guidance for Schools from Chapter 3, so they understand the kind of support they might reasonably expect from their school.

Essential reading: Chapters 1 and 3 of the course handbook (Shotton and Burton, 2008).

Suggested timings for the day:

9.15   Welcome and introduction to the ELSA course.

9.45   Presentation: Emotional Literacy in Schools – slides 1-17

10.45   Tea/coffee.

11.15   Presentation: Emotional Literacy in Schools – slides 18-end.

12.15   Lunch.

1.00   Presentation: Raising Emotional Awareness.

1.45   Getting Started (elaboration of information on handout).

2.15   Planning (group activity).

3.00   Plenary.

3.15   End.

Slides 1-36

Emotional Literacy in Schools

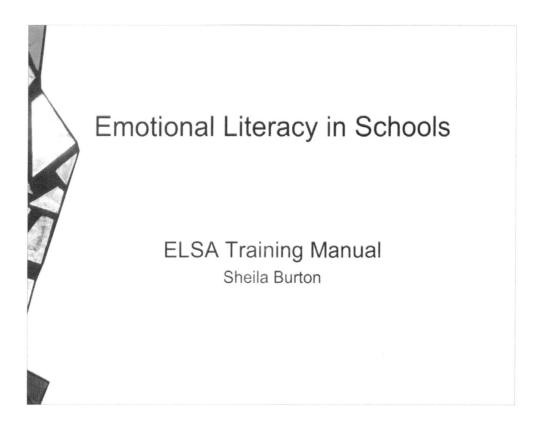

Emotional Literacy in Schools

ELSA Training Manual
Sheila Burton

Facilitator Notes for Slide 1

The facilitator should prepare the following resources for this session:

- A slide show of photographs showing poignant world events to be shown between slides 18 and 19 (as an illustration of the consequences of emotional illiteracy).

- A self-reflection tool to follow presentation (for example, the activity pages EQ Self-test, EQ Self-test Score Sheet and Stop, Start, Continue from Fenman Limited, 2000). This is included as a handout with permission from the publishers.

Aims:

To describe:

- the psychology of emotional literacy.

To consider:

- the importance of emotional literacy
- our own emotional literacy
- the school's role in developing children's emotional literacy.

Facilitator Notes for Slide 2

Explain briefly the aims outlined on this slide.

Ask participants for some initial thoughts on why emotional literacy is an important area for consideration in schools.

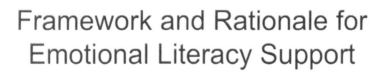

Framework and Rationale for Emotional Literacy Support

- As an inclusive society we all have a responsibility to encourage the emotional wellbeing of all children.

- A child's ability to succeed within a learning environment is enhanced by their emotional wellbeing.

- The emotional wellbeing of children in school is promoted through both its culture and ethos, and the clarity of expectations and purpose.

Facilitator Notes for Slide 3

Emotional literacy support is about helping children to become emotionally well balanced. Today we will be exploring just what emotional literacy means.

Sometimes we hear staff in school say things like, 'We're not social workers. Our job is to teach.'

Life isn't really like that. It doesn't separate out into neat little parcels. The emotional wellbeing of children is everyone's responsibility. Emotionally healthy children will be better learners.

Children thrive in schools that care for the 'whole child'.

Schools have an important role to play in developing well balanced children.

We need to be as clear about how we do this as we are about teaching literacy and numeracy.

Every Child Matters – Outcomes

- Be healthy – emotional health, making healthy choices.
- Stay safe – from bullying, discrimination, ill treatment.
- Enjoy and achieve – enjoy personal and social development.
- Make a positive contribution – to the community.
- Achieve economic wellbeing – ready for employment.

Facilitator Notes for Slide 4

These are the five outcomes of Every Child Matters (DfES, 27.11.04). Emotional Literacy has a part to play in each of these outcomes.

1. Be healthy includes:

- mental and emotional health
- staying sexually healthy
- choosing not to take illegal drugs.

2. Stay safe includes:

- safety from bullying and discrimination
- safety from anti-social behaviour in and out of school
- having security, stability and being cared for.

3. Enjoy and achieve includes:

- attend and enjoy school
- achieve personal and social enjoyment
- enjoy recreation.

4. Make a positive contribution includes:

- engaging in positive and law abiding behaviour in and out of school
- developing self-confidence and dealing successfully with the changes and challenges life brings.

5. Achieve economic wellbeing includes:

- preparing for the world of work by developing personal responsibility and knowing how to relate appropriately to others.

Some Psychological Foundations

- **Self-actualisation** (Maslow 1970)
  – making the most of one's ability and talents.
- **Self-concept** [thinking aspect of self] and
  self-esteem [emotional aspect of self] – (Bandura).
- **Theory of multiple intelligences** (Gardner 1983) – intelligence is more than cognitive ability.
- **Emotional intelligence** (Salovey & Mayer 1990)
  – understanding emotions and managing them effectively.

Facilitator Notes for Slide 5

We will look at some areas of psychology which contribute to our understanding of emotional literacy:

- **Maslow's theory of self-actualisation** (to use a gardening analogy, this might be described as a process of 'blossoming').

- **Self-concept and self-esteem.** Bandura did extensive work in this area. He wrote that, 'People who regard themselves as highly efficacious act, think and feel differently from those who perceive themselves as inefficacious. They produce their own future, rather than simply foretell it.'

- **Gardner's theory of multiple intelligences** – included the intrapersonal and interpersonal domains (self-awareness and awareness of others).

- Leading to work on **emotional intelligence** (initially by Salovey & Mayer but popularised by Daniel Goleman).

How well we manage our emotional life influences our achievements and social success.

We are going to look at each of these areas in a little more detail.

Maslow's Hierarchy of Human Needs

self-actualisation

esteem needs

belongingness & love needs

safety needs

biological & physiological needs

Facilitator Notes for Slide 6

Give out the handout, Maslow's Hierarchy of Human Needs.

Maslow suggested a five-stage hierarchy. He suggested that higher needs could only be met if the lower ones had been met first. There is debate about the extent to which these needs are rigidly hierarchical, but it remains a useful model. It seems to make sense on the basis of experience.

Sometimes you will see extensions to these five stages. That's because others developed Maslow's hierarchy further in the 1970s, adding cognitive needs then aesthetic needs between esteem needs and self-actualisation.

It was modified further in the 1990s adding transcendence needs beyond self-actualisation. Transcendence relates to the need to help others towards self-actualisation.

Activity Linked to Slide 6

Ask participants to discuss how we can impact on all these levels for a child in school.

Even if their background circumstances are difficult, we can make a significant difference. There can be a tendency toward hopelessness amongst school staff because they cannot change a child's home circumstances. However, adversity at home can be offset by quality educational experiences. ELSAs need to focus on what support can be offered in school to meet these needs, not on what isn't happening for children at home.

Reflect and Discuss

- Take a few minutes to think about a child you know in school whose needs may not be adequately met at the lower levels of Maslow's hierarchy.

- What impact is this having on how they manage in school?

Activity Linked to Slide 7

Introduce activity. This will best be done in twos or threes.

Encourage participants to keep their descriptions brief as they could easily become sidetracked into lengthy descriptions of a child's circumstances.

The focus should be on the observable impact on the pupil in school.

(You may find it useful as a comparison to also reflect later on a child who seems to have good self-esteem and be achieving well.)

Self-concept

Different components:

- physical
- academic
- social
- transpersonal.

Facilitator Notes for Slide 8

There are several different components to the self-concept:

Physical – relates to what we look like (height, weight, gender and so on), the kind of clothes we wear, the things we have, the home we live in.

Academic – relates to how well we do in school or how well we learn.

There are two types of academic self-concept:

1. General academic self-concept – how good we are overall.
2. Specific content-related self-concepts – how good we are in maths, English, science and so on.

Social – how we relate to other people.

Transpersonal – how we relate to things outside of ourselves that we can't explain, for example, how we think about the meaning of life. We know, for example, that people who take a religious perspective on that tend to be happier, healthier and less depressed.

Development of Self-concept

- Personal accomplishment.
- Visceral feedback.
- Verbal persuasion.
- Vicarious experiences.

Facilitator Notes for Slide 9

Development of self-concept. We develop and maintain our self-concept through a process of taking action, then reflecting on what we have done and on what others tell us about what we have done. This is a dynamic process – our self-concept can change over time.

Personal accomplishment. The principal component of self-concept is personal accomplishment, which develops the sense of self-efficacy. For children, accomplishments are relative mastery of tasks presented in school, such as reading and maths. An old motto says, 'Nothing breeds success like success.'

Curricula and instructional approaches that allow children to master academic building blocks are essential to:

- the promotion of positive self-concepts
- the creation of a willingness to tackle escalating academic tasks.

Failure leads to negative self-concepts and a reluctance to attempt anything new.

Visceral feedback. These are the messages the body gives us to indicate pleasure, pain, anxiety and so forth. Bodily awareness is needed in order to be aware of our emotional state. Some children are very poor at recognising the signs of bodily change or understanding them. This is often a good starting place for emotional literacy work – raising emotional awareness.

Verbal persuasion. Verbal persuasion is powerful. Praise and encouragement can stimulate accomplishment, but indiscriminate praise is unhelpful. It needs to be genuine or children will see through it. Be aware of hidden messages. Constantly praising effort and progress may have a hidden meaning for a child, ('I'm no good at this. I can only do it with lots of effort.') while praising achievement ('You're good at this.') implies high ability. In our culture, the latter attribution leads to higher self-efficacy than attributions of expended effort (Schunk, 1983).

Vicarious experiences. The final component proposed by Bandura (1986) is vicarious experiences – observing others. We also utilise others to evaluate our own performances. Festinger proposed that social comparison was used to judge self-performance in the absence of objective measures. Schunk (1983) and Bandura (1986) found that children use social comparison to estimate self-efficacy.

Self-esteem

'A person's perceptions regarding himself or herself. These perceptions are formed through experience with and interpretations of one's environment. They are influenced especially by evaluations by significant others, by reinforcements and by attributions on one's own behaviour.'
(Marsh 1990)

Facilitator Notes for Slide 10

Defining the self in relation to the outside world is central to our development. This is a dynamic and fluid process which takes different forms at different times in our lives.

Rogers (1961) recognised it as central to all other forms of learning – people will only learn if they feel that the learning helps to construct or maintain the sense of self. They will reject or block learning that is not consistent with that sense of self. (This helps us to understand why some children may be resistant to praise.)

Sense of positive self-esteem is seen as essential for mental, emotional and social health.

Gordon and Grant (1997) found that one in ten pupils viewed themselves as useless and/or a failure.

Bowlby (1980) noted that children thrive when they have people who provide a warm and approving foundation from which to venture into the world. Essentially this is about being loved unconditionally.

Carers can be so needy themselves that they are unable to provide that unconditional love in the face of a child's negative expression.

Bowlby is renowned for his work on attachment theory.

Discuss

- Think of a child you know with high self-esteem – what would we see?

- Think of a child you know with low self-esteem – what would we see?

Discuss in pairs.

Activity Linked to Slide 11

So how do we make judgments about a child's self-esteem in school? What are the behaviours that cause us to conclude that a child's self-esteem is high or low? Discuss in pairs.

Collate feedback ideas on a flipchart and bring it back on Day 2 when the focus is on self-esteem. These ideas will be revisited.

Theory of Intelligence

1. Visual/spatial.
2. Verbal/linguistic.
3. Logical/mathematical.
4. Bodily/kinaesthetic.
5. Musical/rhythmic.
6. Intrapersonal.
7. Interpersonal.

(Gardner, 1983)

Facilitator Notes for Slide 12

Theory of intelligence – Howard Gardner broadened the concept of intelligence beyond the narrow, traditional view of fixed cognitive ability. He identified seven dimensions. (Although he has since added others.)

Activity Linked to Slide 12

Think about the kinds of occupations that would map on to these areas, for example, what kind of occupations might attract people with high visual/spatial intelligence? Do this as a whole-group discussion.

The last two dimensions are the ones particularly relevant to emotional intelligence.

What is Emotional Intelligence?

Personal Competence

'How we handle ourselves:'

- self-awareness
- self-regulation
- motivation.

Social Competence

'How we handle relationships:'

- empathy
- social skills.

(Goleman, 1998)

Facilitator Notes for Slide 13

Goleman highlighted two corresponding processes within emotional intelligence. (The terms emotional intelligence and emotional literacy tend to be used interchangeably. We will explain our preference for the term emotional literacy later.)

1. The first area is about **how we manage ourselves.**

How aware are we of our own feelings, thought patterns and behaviour?

Are we able to manage these aspects of our life, or are we at times overcome by them?

How motivated are we to learn from our experiences and change unhelpful patterns of feeling, thinking and behaviour into more positive ones?

2. The second area is about **how we manage our interactions with others.**

Can we put ourselves in other people's shoes?

Are we willing and able to adapt our behaviour to take account of other people's feelings and attitudes?

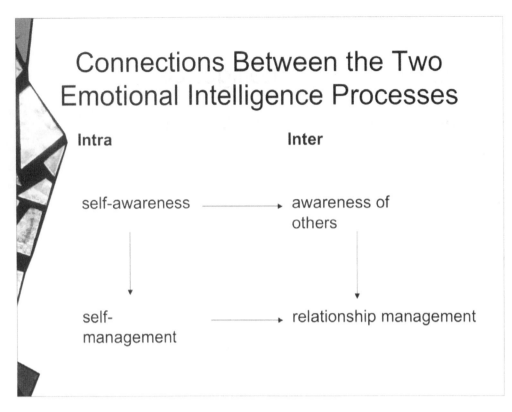

Connections Between the Two Emotional Intelligence Processes

Intra   **Inter**

self-awareness ——————→ awareness of others

self-
management   ——————→ relationship management

This diagram illustrates the relationship between the two areas of **intrapersonal** (within the person) and **interpersonal** (from person to person) intelligence.

Goleman has made significant claims that EI is more important that IQ in determining success.

Emotional Intelligence

'The ability to perceive accurately, appraise and express emotion: the ability to access and/or generate feelings which facilitate thought; the ability to understand emotion and emotional knowledge; the ability to regulate emotions to promote emotional and intellectual growth.'

(Mayer and Salovey 1997)

Facilitator Notes for Slide 15

(Pause to read the definition offered by Mayer & Salovey.)

'Emotional intelligence' tends to be used within the work environment.

'Emotional literacy' (first coined by Steiner, 1984) tends to be used within schools. This is probably to break away from the concept of a fixed level of underlying intelligence that IQ implies. Emotional intelligence is not in any way fixed by genetic factors – it can be developed.

The terms emotional intelligence and emotional literacy can be used interchangeably. We will use the term emotional literacy (EL).

The EL movement has recognised the link between emotion and language. There is a need to help learners to get in touch with their feelings through exploring and developing linguistic competence.

Children with more developed language skills are more emotionally aware.

Activity Linked to Slide 15

Whole-group discussion.

Why might children with better language skills be more emotionally aware?

Discuss briefly. Refer to Mayer and Salovey's definition.

Emotional Literacy

Those who cope well and achieve in their learning are more likely to be able to:

- know and articulate their own feelings
- manage their emotional life, without being overwhelmed by it
- be persistent in the face of difficulties
- show empathy, reading others' emotions
- handle relationships with skill and harmony.

Facilitator Notes for Slide 16

Emotional literacy is about:

- being able to recognise and communicate the range of emotions we experience
- being able to manage (be on top of) those feelings rather than being ruled by them
- being resilient when faced with adversity
- being in tune with the feelings of others
- being able to treat others with sensitivity and respect.

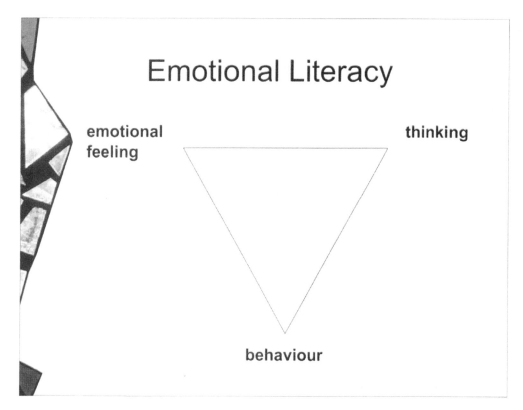

Facilitator Notes for Slide 17

This diagram shows the interplay of three components within emotional literacy:

1. Our affective state (how we are feeling).

2. What we are thinking.

3. How we react to the way we are feeling and the things we are thinking.

Each of these components affect the others.

Self-preservation

- We all have a need to feel significant.
- We will defend our sense of value, self concept or belonging at all costs.
- Our best and worst behaviour is usually very emotional.
- The dramatic consequences of emotional illiteracy are evident all around us.

Activity Linked to Slide 18

Discuss these points briefly in small groups. Invite participants to think of examples that illustrate these statements.

Option: Following this slide, the trainers may like to insert slides containing photos of world events that illustrate the final point. There are many photographic images available on the Internet of wars, terrorist attacks, cruelty and suffering. If a series of images is shown, they will have greater impact without commentary. Scroll through in silence or with some suitable music. The purpose is to provoke personal reflection.

The Human Challenge

'We have learned how to fly to the moon, but we still haven't learned how to walk hand in hand as brothers and sisters.'

(Martin Luther King)

Facilitator Notes for Slide 19

This slide is a link from photos of world events to the here and now.

We may have achieved many amazing technical feats in the last hundred years, but we still struggle to get along with each other.

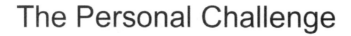

The Personal Challenge

Living with other people, how do I preserve my own sense of self-worth and self-competence… and, at the same time, maintain the self-esteem and self-competence of others?

Facilitator Notes for Slide 20

It's easy to think globally because it's more impersonal. There is no obvious personal cost to making judgements about other people's behaviour.

But emotional literacy has to begin at the level of 'me'.

In seeking to get my own needs met, do I respect the needs and feelings of others? This is at the heart of emotional literacy – self-awareness balanced with awareness of others and our impact upon them.

If we fail to address the personal challenge, how can we ever begin to address the human challenge?

Why is Emotional Literacy Important?

'Developing children as rounded people and active members of the community is at the heart of what schools are about.'

(Estelle Morris in a speech to SCAA Primary Curriculum Conference, June 1997)

Facilitator Notes for Slide 21

This is a quote from Estelle Morris (a previous Secretary of State for Education).

Our educational responsibilities don't begin and end with curriculum targets.

We will always have a responsibility to support the development of 'the whole child'.

Four Foundation Beliefs

1. Positive relationships are vital for brain development and therefore learning.
2. Behaviour is an expression of emotions.
3. Emotions affect both what and how learning takes place.
4. Emotions cannot be separated from the body or the mind.

(Elizabeth Morris, School of Emotional Literacy)

Activity Linked to Slide 22

Discuss briefly in small groups each point on this slide, taking brief feedback between each.

Elizabeth Morris, from the School of Emotional Literacy, suggested that the following four foundational beliefs underpin emotional literacy:

1. The lack of positive relationships will have an adverse effect on brain development, and therefore learning. (Can we think of any evidence for this? Ask delegates to think of any examples. Allow a couple of minutes for small group discussion. If no examples are offered, the obvious one to highlight is the Romanian orphans in children's homes.)

2. Behaviour doesn't occur in isolation – it reflects an emotional state.

(Give time for brief small group discussion about this and invite feedback.)

3. What we learn, and how we learn, are affected by our underlying emotions at the time.

(Can we think of ways in which learning is affected by emotions? Allow another couple of minutes for brief discussion in twos or threes. If feedback is limited, give the example of bereavement, where grief keeps intruding on thoughts and concentration on learning becomes difficult.)

4. Emotions are an integral part of our humanity. Emotions, bodily feelings and thoughts are all interconnected. (We considered this on an earlier slide – the triangle diagram.)

Mental Health Issues

- Mental health problems currently cost UK economy estimated £93 billion every year.

- Mental illness affects more than 25% of the UK population every year.

- By 2020 depression is expected to be most prevalent illness worldwide.

Facilitator Notes for Slide 23

The purpose of the next three slides is to raise awareness of the seriousness of mental health issues in our society, and therefore the need to address emotional and mental wellbeing more effectively from an early age.

Mental Health Issues

More than 140,000 young people in England and Wales are admitted to accident and emergency departments each year because they have tried to kill themselves.

(PAPYRUS – Prevention of Young Suicide)
www.papyrus.org.uk

Facilitator Notes for Slide 24

A statistic about attempted suicides.

Papyrus is a registered charity working towards prevention of suicides in young people (www.papyrus.org.uk).

They provide resources and support for those dealing with suicide, depression or emotional distress.

Mental Health Issues

- In the UK, suicide is now the second most common cause of death (after road accidents) in the 15-24 age group.
- Each year approximately 500 males and 100 females in this age group take their own lives.
- Half of them are not classified as mentally ill.

(PAPYRUS)

Facilitator Notes for Slide 25

Some statistics about actual suicides.

These statistics represent the extreme end of mental health.

Other issues would include depression, drug and alcohol abuse.

Discussion: Reflect for a few minutes in groups of two or three on these statistics and their implications for us.

Academic Achievement

- Children learn more effectively if they are happy in their work, believe in themselves, like their teachers and feel school is supporting them.

- Achievement in school in academic subjects is vital to pupil happiness and self-esteem.

(Gordon and Grant, 1997)

Facilitator Notes for Slide 26

We know that when any of these things change, there is an effect on children's learning.

It's also true that teachers teach most effectively when they are happy in their work, believe in themselves, like their pupils and feel school is supporting them.

When children feel they aren't getting anywhere in terms of learning, their unhappiness and disappointment in themselves is seen in a variety of behaviours from very withdrawn to very challenging (including plenty of strategies for work-avoidance).

Achievement in school is also vital to teacher happiness and self-esteem. Staff need to feel they're doing a good job too.

So while schools can make a contribution to the development of pupil emotional health, the psychology is just as important for teachers.

Benefits of Emotional Literacy Focus in Schools

- When we feel good we learn better.
- Improving emotional literacy raises standards.
- Emotional wellbeing makes learning more enjoyable.
- Improved emotional literacy reduces unnecessary stress.

(Sharp, 2001)

Facilitator Notes for Slide 27

Peter Sharp used to be Principal Educational Psychologist in Southampton and worked with other managers within education to make emotional literacy one of the top priorities in the educational development plan in the city. Why?:

- As we've already said, children learn more effectively when they feel OK.

- If we help children to manage their emotions more effectively and therefore learn better, then we will help to raise standards.

- When children feel better they get more enjoyment out of their learning.

- Developing children's ability to mange their emotions more effectively reduces their stress levels. (Together with Adrian Faupel and Liz Herrick, Peter Sharp has done a lot of work on anger management. We will be looking at this on Day 3.)

More Benefits

- Positive emotions influence concentration, memory, problem-solving and all learning skills.
- Positive relationships enable individuals to break out of dysfunctional patterns.
- Emotional literacy promotes creativity, innovation and leadership.

(Park, J, Antidote 2000)

Facilitator Notes for Slide 28

Similarly, James Park of 'Antidote' – an organisation committed to raising the profile of the emotional literacy agenda – has highlighted particular benefits as:

- improvements in specific skills associated with learning

- empowering individuals to overcome unproductive behaviour patterns

- the promotion of specific characteristics that we may associate with success.

Social Learning Theory

- Children learn behaviour from the models around them.
- Anti-social behaviour can be learned through imitation.
- Pro-social behaviour can be learned through modelling: there must be consistency in the system of rewards and the behaviour of models.

(Bandura,1961)

Facilitator Notes for Slide 29

Bandura's work in the field of social psychology is well-known.

He highlighted the importance of the behaviour children see modelled around them in shaping their own behaviour.

We know that children will imitate poor role-models. Many children who come into our care in school will have experienced and be reproducing some very negative patterns of behaviour.

Nevertheless, schools can be very effective in modelling alternative, more positive, ways of being. (The power is in the 'modelling' more than in the 'teaching'.)

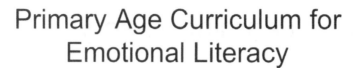

Primary Age Curriculum for Emotional Literacy

- Recognising emotions
  – developing emotional vocabulary.
- Self-esteem
  – developing self-respect.
- Social skills
  – developing interpersonal competence.
- Friendship skills
  – developing interest in others.
- Anger management
  – developing self-regulation.

Facilitator Notes for Slide 30

We've talked about emotional literacy in quite broad terms, but what sort of areas of competence would come under the umbrella term of emotional literacy?

Children experience a full range of emotions, but will not necessarily understand what they are or be able to put them into words. A great deal of work can be done in schools to extend children's emotional vocabulary.

Many children in our schools experience low self-esteem, especially if they find learning or social relationships difficult, and may need help to recognise their unique attributes and value.

The skills of social interaction need to be modelled, and sometimes overtly taught, in order to help children relate effectively both to adults and to other children.

Some children need specific support to develop the kind of skills that enable them to establish and sustain friendships.

Strong emotions can be difficult to handle. Some people have not learned how to keep themselves and other people safe when they feel angry or frustrated.

Refer ELSAs to the SEAL materials that all schools should have. These are aimed at whole-class work, but may contain some useful ideas for ELSAs. The emotions photographs are especially good.

Secondary Age Curriculum for Emotional Literacy

The primary curriculum plus:

- fostering the development of individuality
- encouraging a longer-term view of the student's role in life
- exploration of role
  (student, sibling, offspring, grandchild, friend, citizen)
- forming and maintaining stable relationships
  (friends, peers, teachers, parents)
- empowering young people to ask 'why' questions
- helping them learn to tolerate the ambiguity associated with both good and bad feelings about the same person or thing
  (parents, teachers, school).

(Sharp, 2001)

Facilitator Notes for Slide 31

These are two useful resources:

1. Sharp P. (2001) *Nurturing Emotional Literacy – A practical guide for teachers, parents and those in the caring professions*. London: David Fulton Publishers.

2. Schilling, Dianne (1999) *50 Activities for Teaching Emotional Intelligence. Level III: High School*. California: Innerchoice Publishing.

The Schilling book has 50 activities, mostly based around discussion, some worksheets and some presentations.

Recommended for groups of 8-12 (could be used with larger groups).

Areas covered:

- self-awareness
- managing feelings
- decision-making
- personal responsibility
- self-concept
- empathy
- communications
- group dynamics.

What Do We Need to Do?

- Be good models for appropriate behaviour.
- Raise emotional awareness.
- Reinforce desirable behaviour.
- Teach effective social skills.

Facilitator Notes for Slide 32

These are very brief summary points – not needing to be addressed at length.

We've talked about being and living an emotionally literate lifestyle – setting good examples to the children we work with.

We need to help them to be more aware of the power of emotions so that they can learn to manage them effectively.

We need to specifically recognise and acknowledge good behaviour, increasing pupils' self-awareness and awareness of others.

We need to explicitly teach children the skills they need for relating successfully with others.

What Else do We Need?

- The belief that all children can be helped to improve, whatever their circumstances or starting point.
- A positive problem-solving approach
- Commitment.
- To support each other when the going gets tough.

Facilitator Notes for Slide 33

We need to keep faith with the notion that all things are subject to change. Change may be difficult but nothing is impossible. It is this belief that gives us the resilience to persist in the face of challenge and protects against feelings of helplessness.

When it's hard to see a way through, we need to be able to step back from feelings of hopelessness and be willing to try something different. Statements like, 'We've done everything that could be done,' are self-defeating.

Perseverance to keep going and not give up is vital.

And we need to remember that none of us is superhuman! We need the encouragement of others when things don't seem to be working out. Explain the principle of supervision and that ELSAs will get half-termly group supervision.

But some things won't wait till then. ELSAs need someone in school to talk confidentially with. Ready access to support is essential when listening to children's problems so that you don't become personally overwhelmed.

Discuss in small groups who you will go to for support in ELSA work.

Schools Need Teachers and LSAs Who Can...

- nurture good relationships
- model emotionally literate ways of behaving
- create a calm, positive, orderly atmosphere
- be supportive, encouraging, challenging
- be child-centred
- be inclusive.

Facilitator Notes for Slide 34

In summary then, schools need teachers and LSAs who can:

- gain the respect of children by the respect they show
- manage their own feelings and behaviour in a positive way
- stay calm in the face of challenges and frustrations
- help children – through their support and encouragement – to dare to be different
- see things from the child's perspective
- make every child know they count.

These are the essential qualities of ELSAs.

Self-reflection

- Complete the EQ Self-test.

- Score using the EQ Self-test Score Sheet.

- Consider what this tells you about yourself.

- Plan change using the Stop, Start, Continue activity page.

With thanks to Fenman Limited, for the use of this scale.

(Bagshaw, M. Using Emotional Intelligence at Work Fenman Limited (2000))

Facilitator Notes for Slide 35

Introduce the Fenman EQ Self-test as an opportunity for participants to assess their own competencies.

Explain that this is a confidential process that participants can do in their own time. Either allow time in the session or suggest as a 'take home'.

Give out the following activity pages:

- EQ Self-test.
- EQ Self-test Score Sheet.
- Stop, Start, Continue.

Activity Linked to Slide 35

Complete the EQ Self-test.

Score using the EQ Self-test Score Sheet. Consider what this tells you about yourself.

Plan change using the Stop, Start, Continue activity page.

Priorities

'A hundred years from now it will not matter what my bank account was, the sort of car I drove… but the world may be different because I was important in the life of a child.'

(Sharp, 2001)

Activity Linked to Slide 36

Discuss with the participants the importance of their new role.

Ask for some feedback about what they will particularly remember from this session.

Maslow's Hierarchy of Human Needs

Stage 1

Everyone needs food and drink, warmth, shelter and sleep to function effectively. The quality of provision for these basic needs may affect children's behaviour and learning.

Stage 2

The next level of need is safety. This encompasses protection, security, order and limits. Ideally children need a safe and secure environment in the home, the classroom and in the playground. As long as they feel safe somewhere, they can generally cope. However their personal development will be inhibited if they feel unsafe. It isn't just about physical safety. Verbal bullying, for example, can undermine a child's sense of safety.

Stage 3

After safety comes the need for a sense of belonging. This arises out of being loved and valued within the family, and from the enjoyment of friendships beyond the family. Some children feel unloved at home and isolated at school, and this too will hinder their development.

Stage 4

Esteem needs relate to achievement, status, responsibility and reputation. Everyone needs to be able to feel good about themselves and receive recognition, attention and appreciation. Without a sense of belonging and of being valued by others, people find it hard to value themselves and receive affirmation from those around them. This is what we mean by self-esteem.

Stage 5

Lastly in Maslow's hierarchy comes self-actualisation, or personal growth and fulfillment. We need opportunities to develop all our inner talents and abilities. All children and adults must be given chances to experiment with their own ideas and feel free to attempt their `best'. Poor self-esteem undermines the courage to experiment and develop your potential. This relates to Bandura's work on self-efficacy. Self-efficacy is feelings of competency, upon which self-esteem is based.

Fenman EQ – Self-test

Indicate below how much each statement is like you:

Often   - O
Usually   - U
Sometimes   - S
Occasionally - Oc
Rarely   - R

1. I know which things in my past influence my emotional reactions today. ☐

2. When we're working to a deadline, I can feel relaxed and make it enjoyable and productive for everyone. ☐

3. I give honest, direct and respectful feedback when I feel someone is behaving in an unhelpful way. ☐

4. I make sure I find the time to praise people when they've made a good contribution. ☐

5. I listen carefully to try to understand the other's point of view and how they're feeling. ☐

6. I can hold back hostile thoughts in a disagreement, even though I would like to 'blast' them. ☐

7. I feel comfortable sharing my knowledge and experience with my colleagues. ☐

8. I can build good support networks to help me personally and professionally. I ask for support when I need it. ☐

9. I manage conflict by seeking common ground. I don't allow bad feelings to fester. ☐

10. I readily defer present rewards for future goal achievement. ☐

11. I feel comfortable learning anew, and letting go of old ideas and ways of doing things. ☐

12. I can control anxiety to avoid getting stuck. ☐

Day 1

13. I lead a balanced lifestyle. ☐

14. I notice when my body is telling me I need to relax or energise myself, and I do it. ☐

15. When I start to have negative, defeatist thoughts, I can replace them with positive thoughts that motivate me. ☐

16. I can sustain optimism in the face of repeated disappointment. ☐

17. I regularly step back from today's urgent demands to remind myself of where I want to be, and what I need to do to get there. ☐

18. I manage anger by putting things in perspective and keeping calm. ☐

19. I avoid feeling helpless in frustrating circumstances by focusing on what I have control over. ☐

20. I act on the belief that I can choose a different way. It's not 'just the way I am'. ☐

21. I pick up subtle verbal and non-verbal signals that show how people are feeling underneath the surface. ☐

22. I can handle rejection because my self-esteem is strong. ☐

23. I can reframe, or find alternative ways of viewing, a bad experience. ☐

24. Others would describe me as having lots of drive. ☐

25. I state my concerns without anger or passivity when I am being excluded. ☐

26. My personal vision and values keep me focused in times of greatest difficulty. ☐

27. I avoid procrastinating and take decisive action after considering my options. ☐

28. I sense out and explore opportunities. ☐

29. I am able to take calculated risks without worrying too much about the choices I've made. ☐

30. I don't just sit and react to events. I take control of my own future. ☐

Day 1

Fenman EQ – Self-test Score Sheet

Score your responses as follows:

Often	4
Usually	3
Sometimes	2
Occasionally	1
Rarely	0

No.		TOTALS:
1		
2		
3		
4		
5		
6		
7		
8		
9		
10		
11		
12		
13		
14		
15		
16		
17		
18		
19		
20		
21		
22		
23		
24		
25		
26		
27		
28		
29		
30		

Day 1

Fenman EQ – Self-test Score Sheet (cont)

N.B. This questionnaire has been designed to challenge your thinking about Emotional Intelligence. It is not a standardised psychometric instrument and shouldn't in any way be used to categorise, select or label anyone.

Interpretation

Creative tension	Managing the tension between dealing with the present and creating the future.
Active choice	Being proactive and not procrastinating or worrying about choices you've made.
Resilience under pressure	Managing pressure positively.
Empathic relationships	Building relationships of trust and credibility.
Self-awareness and self-control	Knowing what you're feeling and moderating your internal responses.

Any score of 18 or above on any of the five competencies indicates that you excel in that particular aspect of Emotional Intelligence (although it would be useful to check your self-rating with ratings by others who work with you).

12-17 indicates a strong foundation for development.

0-11 indicates that you may need to explore the particular competence in some depth and to find ways of building that particular aspect of Emotional Intelligence.

Any individual item rated 2 or below may be an important area for you to work on. Consider how much benefit you will gain if you invest time and energy in moving the rating up to a 3 or 4. Now choose up to five items from the EQ self-test that you feel are important for you to work on. Discuss with your colleagues what you will do to strengthen these areas.

Fenman Stop, Start, Continue

I intend to stop...

I intend to start...

I intend to continue...

Day 1

Slides 1-11

Raising Emotional Awareness

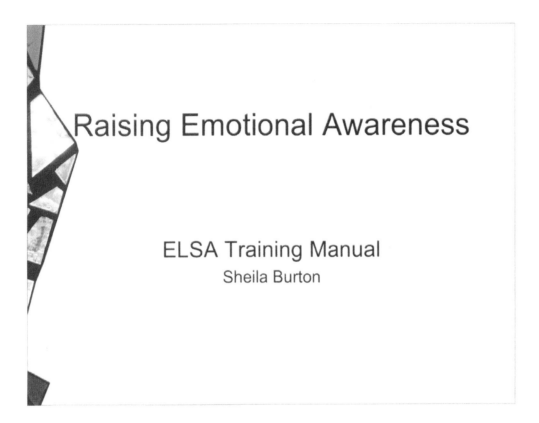

This is often a good place for ELSAs to start when working with children. It is always worth checking out children's understanding of emotions.

We need to find out whether children can differentiate between the different feelings they experience. They will certainly experience a range of emotions but may not understand what those feelings are communicating.

We need to ensure children develop an adequate vocabulary to express their feelings.

Aims

The aims are to:

- identify key questions when assessing a pupil's emotional awareness

- recognise the ambiguity of facial expression

- suggest a variety of approaches and resources to develop emotional awareness.

Facilitator Notes for Slide 2

This module considers ways of checking out children and young people's degree of emotional awareness.

Facial expressions can be interpreted differently and once we move beyond basic broad categories of expression there are many subtle variations to interpret.

A rich variety of resources can be drawn upon to support work on identifying and naming emotions.

Assessing Emotional Awareness

Question 1:

Does the child express a range of emotions?

Some children present as emotionally 'flat'.

There are some key questions we might ask when preparing to work with a child.

Do we recognise a range of emotional expression in that child? Can we tell how they are feeling from their facial expressions, body posture, tone of voice?

Activity Linked to Slide 3

Can you think of a child or young person who rarely, if ever, displays any emotion?

What impact do you think this has on you, and on their peers, in relating to them?

Assessing Emotional Awareness

Question 2:

Does the child recognise emotions in other people?

Recognition of facial expressions, body posture and tone of voice.

Facilitator Notes for Slide 4

If the child communicates a range of emotions within him/herself, does he or she also have the capacity to distinguish between the same emotions displayed in other people?

This will involve not only recognition of facial expressions, but also a person's posture and movements, as well as their tone of voice. Each of these aspects is a potential area of focus within ELSA work on emotions.

Recognising Emotional Expression

- Look at handout entitled 'Emotional Expression'.

- Would you have recognised these emotions as labelled?

- What else might some of these expressions indicate?

Activity Linked to Slide 5

We may not all read expressions the same way. Some can be more ambiguous than others.

Ask participants if they agree with all the labels attached to the expressions on the handout.

If not, what emotional label might they have assigned to the expression?

Assessing Emotional Awareness

Question 3:

Does the child have the vocabulary to label different emotions?

For example, happy, sad, angry, frightened.

Facilitator Notes for Slide 6

Does the child use emotional labels to describe their feelings or can they only tell us how they feel by the way they behave?

In the absence of easy access to language for describing and explaining feelings, a child is only left with the option of expressing their feelings through the way they act and react. Whether they show acting out or withdrawn behaviour, this communicates something of how they feel about themselves and what is happening to them.

It is often the behaviour itself that troubles or concerns us, as the behaviour tends to compound the difficulties a child is experiencing. Behaviour has an immediacy about it, but may mask the underlying emotional difficulties by focusing our attention in the wrong place.

In the earlier years of school, adults may compound the problem of limited vocabulary by using a restricted emotional vocabulary themselves. A teacher, for example, may say they feel 'sad' that a child's guinea pig has died but also 'sad' when a child has hurt another child or 'sad' that the rain has prevented them from going out. Alternatives such as 'cross' and 'disappointed' might be more accurate descriptions of the teacher's feelings.

Emotions

Basic Emotions

- Happy
- Sad
- Frightened
- Angry

Additional Emotions

- Lonely
- Worried
- Excited
- Bored
- Proud
- Sorry
- Surprised/shocked
- Disgusted

Facilitator Notes for Slide 7

The four basic emotions suggested here are a good starting place for feelings work with young children, but also with older children who show little understanding of emotional expression.

The list on the right is not exhaustive, but represents a wide range of common emotions. If a young person's vocabulary is not extended, they will use inaccurate descriptors of how they are feeling. Many children, for example, will say they are 'bored' or that something is 'boring' when perhaps they feel anxious, uncertain, disappointed or scared.

Expanding Emotional Vocabulary

- Happy/glad/pleased/content.
- Sad/upset/fed-up/disappointed.
- Frightened/scared/terrified.
- Angry/cross/mad/furious/stressed.
- Lonely/alone/left out.
- Worried/anxious/nervous.
- Excited/thrilled.

Facilitator Notes for Slide 8

There is more than one way to describe any particular feeling and as children get older we will want to expand their range of labels for core feelings. Feelings can be placed along a continuum of intensity, and a more advanced exercise might be to ask a pupil to arrange a series of feelings words in order from most mild to most intense, for example, irritated, cross, angry, livid, furious. (There will be room for some difference of interpretation in this exercise.)

These different words express varying intensity of feeling or subtle differences in context.

Developing Emotional Awareness

Use a variety of approaches.

- Games & activities.
- Stories.
- Pictures.
- Film.
- Puppets.
- Drawings.
- Role–plays.
- Keeping a 'feelings diary'.

Facilitator Notes for Slide 9

There is a great range of published resources that are useful for supporting work on emotions. Children with limited language skills will not learn best by simply being talked to. Illustrations, practical activities and experiential learning will be of far greater impact.

Successful ELSA programmes will draw on a variety of materials and approaches, matched to age and emotional development, to support this work. While most younger children love stories, older children will enjoy watching video or film clips. Turning the sound down will focus them on postural and behavioural cues.

Role-play is an effective way of developing empathy with other people's feelings by adopting alternative roles.

Activity Linked to Slide 9

In small groups, ask participants to discuss approaches they might use to help pupils become more attuned to emotional expression.

This discussion is aimed at stimulating creativity in planning ELSA sessions on emotional awareness.

Useful Resources

- Face Your Feelings.
- A Box Full of Feelings.
- All About Me.
- The Feelings Diary.
- Draw On Your Emotions.
- Mr Men books, for example, Mr Happy.

Facilitator Notes for Slide 10

Details of these and other resources can be found in Chapter 10 of *Emotional Wellbeing: An Introductory Handbook* (Shotton & Burton, 2008).

Useful Sources for Resources

- Incentive Plus educational catalogue
- www.bandapilot.org.uk for DfES SEAL materials
- www.nelig.com
- www.senteacher.org
- www.mes-english.com
- www.do2learn.com

Facilitator Notes for Slide 11

Here are a few useful places to look for resources to support work on emotions (and other aspects of emotional literacy).

The websites are not all primarily on emotional literacy but those that are more general have some specific resources on emotional awareness.

Emotional Expression

Afraid

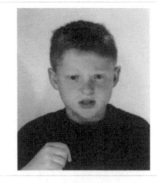

Angry

Happy

Hurt

Moody

Sad

Shy

Upset

Day 1

Feelings

Here are suggestions for children who have difficulties in identifying and expressing feelings. Some of these activities can be carried out in a class/group situation and some require an individual focus.

- Generate words associated with a range of feelings in class. This will provide a range of vocabulary appropriate to the child's age group.

- Use a list to classify, either individually or in a group, which can then provide a framework for more detailed work.

- Explore meanings, non-verbal cues, for example, facial expression, posture, gesture, tone of voice and so on, use pictorial material, including picture story books, mime and role-play.

- In stories, emphasise the feelings of different characters, particularly where there are different feelings about an event/behaviour and so on. Try to explore how a character would respond if she takes notice of the feelings of someone else. It would be useful to provide some other options for the child to choose from, which could be written down if appropriate.

- Explore the child's own feelings about particular 'safe' events. Consider using a rating scale format which is visual and does not necessarily require a detailed verbal response from the child. When established, this format can be used for looking at more difficult individual feelings.

- Look at ways of making others feel good about themselves. Emphasise the small things we often take for granted, for example, the smile, friendly greeting, getting something for someone else, helping out, sharing, asking someone who is left out to join in, putting an arm around someone who is upset. Reflect on a regular basis with the child/group what he has done on that day within this framework. These could be recorded as 'I' statements in a special book, to promote self-esteem.

- Increase explicit awareness of own and others' feelings in paired activities, for example, verbalise feelings about:

  - how well turn-taking was achieved

  - playing someone else's choice of game as well as your own in a turn-taking situation

  - how it was agreed who would do what on a shared task, which can be play- or work-focused.

Emphasise the importance of finding ways for both partners to 'feel good' and enjoy the activity/game. Also emphasise the non-verbal cues which tell us how we can tell what someone else is feeling.

- Use natural opportunities to talk about feelings, particularly where there are different feelings about an event/happening/request and so on.

Jo Birbeck Hampshire Educational Psychology Service

Day 1

Getting Started

Practical Issues

- Your school has agreed to release you for the equivalent of one day each week to carry out ELSA work. This may be in a block or at set times during the week. For some smaller schools this may be a shorter time (for example, half a day per week). It will be important for you to find out what time has been allocated. It may be that you do not use all the allocated time initially but that you will fairly quickly build up to using the whole time available.

- Your school has agreed to make some money available to purchase some resources for you to use. It will be important to find out if they have already purchased them and, if not, order some resources to use so you can make your sessions varied and fun. It will be useful to look at existing resources your school may already have, as well as developing some homemade games and activities.

- You will need a copy of Shotton, G. and Burton, S. (2008) Emotional Wellbeing: An introductory handbook. London: Optimus Education and your school has agreed to buy a copy of this.

- The length of each session will depend on the child. For a younger pupil, 20 minutes may be enough, whereas an older pupil may benefit from a session of an hour. You will need to judge this. You may find it helps younger pupils to have several shorter sessions each week.

- It is helpful to set some clear goals. Once these have been achieved, you may decide to stop sessions with that pupil and allow time for them to consolidate and generalise these skills. Goals may be achieved within half a term or may take far longer.

- You will need an appropriate place to work with some privacy and quiet but not too isolated.

- You will need to plan the best time to work with each pupil (not during their favourite lesson!) and negotiate with relevant staff.

Parent/Carer Involvement

- It is good practice to inform parents/carers.

- Written consent is desirable.

- Schools usually send a letter to parents/carers to suggest their child would benefit from ELSA support, inviting them to contact the school to discuss further if they have any concerns or would like to find out more about the work carried out. Sometimes it would be more appropriate to approach parents/carers in person.

Day 1

- It is good practice to feed back progress to parents/carers at appropriate stages. This could coincide with IEP or IBMP reviews. It will be useful for you to talk to appropriate school staff to plan how best to do this.

Session Planning and Recording

- A good session has pace and variety.
- Start by welcoming the pupil, and warm up with a neutral game or activity.
- Recap from the previous session to see if they have remembered/understood the information. Ask them what they learned from the last session, and find out if they have followed through any actions you had agreed.
- Carry out a range of activities to achieve the objectives for that session. These can include games, puppets, making something with a younger child, looking at or sorting pictures, drawing and so on. It is important not to base it all around pen and paper exercises, but an activity page can be useful to consolidate the activities. Often your role is to facilitate learning by allowing the pupil to experience and talk about the activities.
- You may want to ask the pupil to try something before the next session. This could be something for them to notice during the week, something for them to record, or a new approach to use.
- Finish a session with a fun, cool-down activity or a favourite game, and ensure they are emotionally ready to return to their lessons. Always try to leave the pupil wanting more, not asking when the session is finishing!
- It is important to have evidence of the work you are carrying out to share with the teacher/SENCO/parents/Ofsted, and so you can review and evaluate the work.
- A planning sheet for each session allows you to record the objective for the session, resources needed, activities you plan to carry out, and reflections after the session about how successful it was, and noting anything for the next session. A sample planning sheet is available as a handout or you may prefer to design your own to suit you.
- You may wish to increase pupil involvement and engagement by including pupils in setting targets and in reviewing their achievements.
- If a pupil is unco-operative with you:

You could finish the session early and suggest you continue the following week. You may wish to acknowledge that you feel the pupil is not ready to work with you on this occasion, without blaming or punishing in any way. If the session is abandoned, ensure they do not receive negative feedback about this from the teacher when they return to class.

If the pupil is wishing to control the session or set her own agenda, you may be able to negotiate a little or give a controlled choice of activity.

If the pupil is out of control, get help.

Day 1

Confidentiality

- It is important to build a trusting relationship.

- You may need to reassure the pupil that you will not be sharing what they tell you with anyone else without their permission, unless they say something that means they are not safe. You would then need to pass that information on.

- Sometimes you may think it would be helpful to share information with a child's teacher or parent. If so, talk about this with the child. Check out whether they would be happy for you to do this and whether there is anything they would not want you to say.

Child Protection Issues

- It is important for you to make yourself aware of the child protection procedures within your school. If the pupil starts to disclose and you have not discussed confidentiality with them, it will be important to stop them to explain that you may need to tell someone else if what they are about to say means they are not safe. It is important for you to know who the Child Protection Liaison Officer (CPLO) is in your school. If a child does disclose information, you will need to record the information accurately as soon as possible and give a copy to the CPLO, who will then decide on appropriate action. You may also wish to enlist on a Child Protection Awareness course.

- In recording information, keep your account factual and quote the child's own words where possible. When a child discloses it is important to listen carefully and dispassionately. Be aware that any reaction of shock may cause the child to feel uncomfortable about continuing to confide in you. Avoid asking leading questions. It is not your responsibility to investigate the issues or interrogate the pupil. There are trained professionals (social workers and police officers) who will undertake this role if the pupil is deemed to be at risk.

- For your own safety it is important to use commonsense about where you work with youngsters. Although you need a quiet area, it may be sensible to leave the door open, or find somewhere which is quiet but with other people nearby.

ELSA Referral Form

Request for Emotional Literacy Support

Name: ....

DoB: ....

Year group: ....

Background information: ....

Prioritising key areas to target:

	Skill	Ability				
		1 very poor	2	3	4	5 very good
Emotional Awareness	Ability to recognise how they feel.					
	Ability to say how they feel and why.					
Social Skills	Making eye contact.					
	Taking turns.					
	Speaking in a pleasant tone of voice.					
	Asking for help.					
	Asking for help.					
	Paying attention when spoken to.					
Friendship Skills	Ability to initiate friendships.					
	Ability to maintain friendships.					
	Understanding what friends do and do not do.					
Self-esteem	Ability to identify strengths.					
	Ability to accept praise.					
	Ability to accept constructive criticism.					
	Perseverance for tasks they find difficult.					
	Ability to cope with new experiences/ change.					
Anger Management	Ability to recognise when feeling angry.					
	Knowledge and use of strategies to help calm down when angry.					
	Ability to seek adult help when angry/ frustrated.					

Day 1

Aims

By the end of 7-10 weeks of ELSA support we hope that ....
(name) will be able to:

1.

2.

3.

Session Planning Guidelines for ELSAs

Proactive Support

While ELSAs may often be called upon to deal with the fallout from incidents in school, this should be recognised as additional to their role and not their principal function. ELSAs have been established to deliver planned programmes of support designed to increase the emotional literacy skills of the children and young people with whom they work. This is proactive, not reactive work.

Programme Aims

When agreeing to work with a pupil, it is important to set clear programme aims. This should be done in conjunction with the member of staff requesting ELSA involvement or with your line manager. These may be identified by asking the question, 'By the end of my involvement, what is it that you hope this pupil will be able to do that they are not able to do at present?' You may identify up to three aims in this way, but more than that is likely to be unrealistic. These aims should be like SMART targets on Individual Education Plans:

- Small.
- Measurable.
- Achievable.
- Realistic.
- Time-limited.

The time frame within which you expect them to be achieved would generally be between half a term and a term. If a programme lasts a lot longer than this it probably indicates an absence of clear and realistic targets. Once the programme aims have been completed it may be appropriate to provide some ongoing review arrangements so that the pupil has some continued but reduced support while generalising new skills, for example, a brief weekly review or a longer session once every few weeks.

Session Objectives

Each session should have an objective – a small step on the way to achieving the programme aims. This helps you to ensure that your sessions with a pupil are purposeful. On occasion a pupil may arrive with an issue or need that supersedes your planned objective, causing you to deviate from your session plan. It is responsive to do so, and it would then be appropriate to record this on the session plan, noting what you did instead, so that you can return to the original plan in a subsequent session as appropriate. If you continually deviate from the plan it again suggests that your intervention lacks clear aims.

Day 1

Session Planning Guidelines for ELSAs (cont)

Format of Session Plan

This should fit within one page. It is helpful to list any resources you will need for the session and briefly outline the activities. A good session is likely to include an initial warm-up (for example, review how the pupil is that day or how their week has gone), a brief recap of the previous session to check that the pupil can remember what she learned, a simple explanation of the objective for the current session, an engaging learning activity, a summary of the main points and a take-away activity. This last part may simply be a request to notice something specific in the week ahead or to try out a strategy that has been discussed. Following a brief written plan helps ensure purpose and pace within sessions. It is helpful at the end of the session to add a few brief evaluative comments to this sheet of what went well or anything you want to remember to inform future session plans. The completed session plans then form a record of involvement that provides accountability for the time spent in support of a young person. They are also a useful aide memoir when liaising with other staff or with parents/carers.

Day 1

ELSA Session Plan

Pupil name: ....

Date: ....

Session objective ....

....

....

Resources: ....

....

....

Activities: ....

....

....

Evaluation: ....

....

....

Name/signature of ELSA: ....

Day 1

Letter to Parents/Carers (Sample)

School name and address

Parents/Carers address

Date

Dear ....

We have noticed in school that ...(name of child) ... is having difficulty with
.... (specify areas of concern, for example, making friends, initiating
conversations with others, playing with others at playtime, managing angry feelings, in
class).

We would like to help ... (name of child) ... to make progress in this/these area(s).
Mr/Mrs/Miss/Ms .... (our Emotional Literacy Support Assistant) has
had training to help children with these kinds of difficulties. We would like ... (name of
child) ... to spend some time each week working with Mr/Mrs/Miss/Ms ....

We hope you are in agreement with this support. If you have any questions or you think
there is anything it would be helpful for us to know about before starting this work,
please come and talk to me or leave a message with the school office for me to ring you.

You will also be welcome to arrange a time during the next few weeks to come into
school and talk with Mr/Mrs/Miss/Ms .... and me about the work he/
she is doing with ... (name of child).

Yours sincerely

Class teacher

Enclosed: information for parents/carers.

Day 1

Information for Parents/Carers (Primary Sample)

An ELSA (Emotional Literacy Support Assistant) is a member of staff who is trained to support children in the development of their emotional literacy.

What is emotional literacy?
- Understanding and coping with the feelings about ourselves and others.
- Developing high self-esteem and positive interactions with others.
- Being emotionally literate helps children focus better on their learning.

Some of the areas the ELSA may work on:
- Recognising emotions.
- Self-esteem.
- Social skills.
- Friendship skills.
- Anger management.
- Loss and bereavement.

How does the ELSA work?
- A regular slot during the school week for 30-45 minutes.
- Sessions can be individual or in small groups and tailored to the child's individual needs.
- Sessions are fun and might include role-play, puppets, board games, art and craft and stories.
- They include time to talk.
- A pupil's progress will be reviewed on a half-termly basis.

As a parent/carer, how can you help?
- By informing the class teacher if there are any issues that may be affecting your child.
- Please feel welcome to contact your child's teacher or the ELSA if you have any questions.

The ELSA in your school is ....

Day 1

Day 2

Content and Plan

PowerPoint Presentation – Self-esteem (slides and notes)

Supporting Documents:

1. Building Blocks of Self-esteem – Positive Descriptors – training activity (Linked to Slide 22)

2. Building Blocks of Self-esteem – Rating Scales – training activity (Linked to slides 22 and 24)

3. Practical Ideas and Activities to Support Sequential Development of Self-esteem – training activity (Linked to Slide 23)

4. Building Blocks of Self-esteem – A Focus on Developing Selfhood

5. Building Blocks of Self-esteem – A Focus on Developing Affiliation

PowerPoint Presentation – Active Listening and Communication Skills (slides and notes)

Supporting Documents:

1. Observation – Developing a Shared Understanding and Active Listening Skills – training activity (Linked to Slide 29)

2. Personal Observation and Reflection – training activity (Linked to Slide 30)

3. Active Listening – Using Language to Help the Speaker – handout summarising active listening skills

Day 2

Content and Plan

Subsequent days of training should all begin with a review of how things have progressed for the trainee ELSAs since the previous training day – what they have managed to do so far and any difficulties they have encountered. The purpose of this is for the trainers to monitor progress in implementation of the project in the schools represented, and for them to assist in problem-solving any barriers to implementation. It is important that ELSAs begin working with one or two pupils as soon as they can so that they can put their learning into practice immediately and identify any issues with which they might need support. The training days provide an opportunity for the early support they are bound to need in developing a new role.

The main focus for this second day of training is self-esteem. This has been selected as an early topic because a high proportion of pupils who receive ELSA support are likely to have some self-esteem needs, whether they are youngsters whose behaviour is challenging or those who are more withdrawn. It is a very broad concept and the training module identifies different areas of esteem needs by drawing on a model of self-esteem developed by Michele Borba (1989). This enables more focused support to be offered, tailored to the specific needs of particular pupils.

The focus for the afternoon is on some of the basic counseling skills needed by ELSAs to establish good communication with the pupils they support. While it is assumed that the trainees have been selected by their schools because they have good rapport with children, making explicit the active listening and communication skills helps them to identify personal strengths and areas for further development.

A short plenary session is suggested at the end of each day to check on how the trainees are feeling, give any necessary notices and inform them of the reading they need to do following the session to complement the training they have received that day. This is also an opportunity to complete evaluation forms.

Essential reading: Chapters 2 and 4 of the course handbook, Emotional Wellbeing, (Shotton and Burton, 2008).

Suggested timings for the day:

9.15   Review of progress.

9.45   Presentation: Self-esteem – slides 1-14.

10.45   Tea/coffee.

11.15   Presentation: Self-esteem – slides 15-25.

12.15   Lunch.

1.00   Presentation: Active Listening and Communication Skills.

3.00   Plenary.

3.15   End.

Slides 1-25

Self-esteem

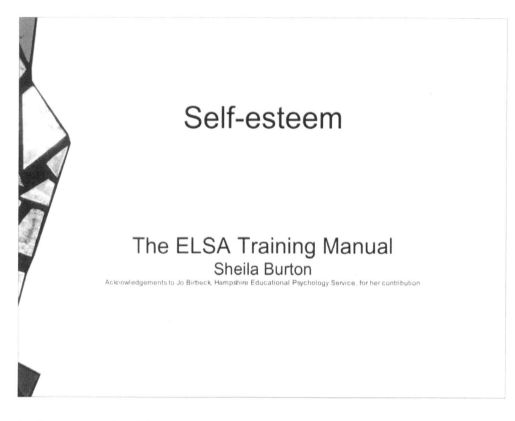

Self-esteem

The ELSA Training Manual

Sheila Burton

Acknowledgements to Jo Birbeck, Hampshire Educational Psychology Service, for her contribution

Facilitator Notes for Slide 1

The resources to be prepared for this session are:

- Building Blocks of Self-esteem – Positive Descriptors (linked to slide 22).

- Building Blocks of Self-esteem – Rating Scales (linked to slide 22 and 24).

- Practical Ideas and Activities to Support Sequential Development of Self-esteem (linked to slide 23).

Aims

The aims are to:

- understand what is meant by self-esteem
- understand the importance of self-esteem
- recognise some key components of self-esteem
- start to use the building blocks of self-esteem model to guide our focus in raising self-esteem.

Facilitator Notes for Slide 2

Self-esteem is a very broad concept and in this session we look at what we mean by self-esteem and why it's an important area of focus.

We identify specific aspects of self-esteem because it is not a unitary concept.

By identifying different facets we can then look at how to address them in a more targeted way.

If I Had My Child to Raise All Over Again…

I'd finger-paint more, and point the finger less.
I'd do less correcting and more connecting.
I'd take my eyes off my watch, and watch with my eyes.
I would care to know less, and know to care more.
I'd take more hikes and fly more kites.
I'd stop playing serious, and seriously play.

Facilitator Notes for Slide 3

Give time for trainees to read this and the next slide, and perhaps allow a few moments for them to comment about the content with the person next to them.

If I had ... (cont'd)

I would run through more fields and gaze at more stars.

I'd do more hugging and less tugging.

I'd be firm less often, and affirm much more.

I'd build self-esteem first, and the house later.

I'd teach less about the love of power, and more about the power of love.

(Loomans, 1994)

Facilitator Notes for Slide 4

This poem comes from a book by Diane and Julia Loomans (1994) called Full Esteem Ahead: One hundred ways to teach values and build self-esteem for all ages.

Self-concept

An umbrella term that incorporates:

- **self-image** – ideas we have about our appearance, abilities and attributes
- **ideal-self** – the picture we build up of how we ought to be
- **self-esteem** – our evaluation of self in relation to ideal-self.

Facilitator Notes for Slide 5

The purpose of this slide is to explain the difference between the terms self-concept and self-esteem.

Self-concept is an umbrella term that incorporates self-image, ideal-self and self-esteem.

Self-image

The earliest impressions of self-image are mainly those of body-image.

These are supplemented by the sense of being loved or not loved, being clever or stupid (conveyed by verbal and non-verbal messages from others).

These ideas are acquired and influenced by how we perceive ourselves to be valued by those around us, then later by our own evaluations of our competence.

Ideal-self

This develops from the comments and value-judgements of the most significant people in our lives. It is the picture we build up of the ideal attributes and characteristics we should strive to possess – in other words, the standards we set for our lives.

Self-esteem

This is a value judgement about the self. It depends upon the discrepancy between our own self-image and our ideal-self.

If our self-image is poor, then there is little hope of ever attaining our ideal-self and our self-esteem is low.

But if our self-image incorporates acceptable physical appearance, competence in many areas and attributes we feel are valued, then our self-esteem will be high.

Self-esteem

Self-esteem is a combination of:

- a general sense of liking ourselves
- being happy with the way we are and the way we live our lives
- judgements about our competence in areas of importance to us.

Facilitator Notes for Slide 6

Self-esteem, then, is about our opinion of ourselves.

The importance we attach to different areas of competence is likely to vary through our lives.

Children with high self-esteem have been found to discount the importance of areas where they are less competent, for example, a child with high self-esteem who is good at sport may not be so concerned at poorer academic performance.

Children with low self-esteem are unable to do this. They are dismayed by any difficulties they experience and so maintain a large discrepancy between their self-image and their ideal-self.

We all seek confirmation of who we are (our self-concept) to sustain stability.

Children with low self-esteem note negative comments that confirm their own view of themselves but fail to 'hear' positive comments because they do not believe such comments relate to them.

Why is Self-esteem Important?

It affects the ability to:

- learn
- build friendships
- deal with difficulties
- cope with change
- achieve potential.

Facilitator Notes for Slide 7

Children don't learn well when they feel bad about themselves.

Friendships are built on mutual respect. If children don't respect and like themselves, they find it difficult to respect and like others.

Children who feel OK about themselves have greater resilience when faced with difficult challenges.

Children who feel OK about themselves are less threatened by change.

Remember Maslow's hierarchy of human needs from Day 1? Developing positive self-esteem is one of the foundations that paves the way for realising potential (self-actualisation).

Cycle of Success
Increase self-esteem and pupils will:

✓ pay attention more *as more attention is paid to them*

✓ become more responsible *as they have been responded to more*

✓ become more achievement orientated *as their basic needs have been met*

✓ become more understanding of others *as they have been helped to understand themselves*

✓ discover a love of learning *as they learn to love and be loved*

Facilitator Notes for Slide 8

This slide illustrates the link between meeting pupils' needs and enabling them to develop socially, emotionally and intellectually.

Allow time for participants to read the slide.

Activity Linked to Slide 8

In small groups ask participants to talk about their initial reactions to these points.

Do they ring true?

Do they know pupils who have made progress when they have begun to experience the parts in italics?

Self-esteem in Schools

Low self-esteem is a key factor in behaviour problems and poor academic achievement but:

- is it addressed in school behaviour plans?
- is it discussed with parents/carers?
- is it addressed in IEPs?
- is it too broad a category?
- is it measured (pre- and post-intervention)?

Facilitator Notes for Slide 9

In schools, children are often identified as having low self-esteem. What is less clear is whether this area of need is then effectively targeted.

These questions are posed to encourage participants to reflect on practice in their own schools:

- Does the school behaviour policy consider the issue of promoting positive self-esteem?

- At individual progress reviews, are ways of raising self-esteem discussed or is the discussion always performance-focused?

- How often do children's Individual Education Plans include targets and strategies to build self-esteem?

- When children are thought to have very low self-esteem, is any attempt made to use self-esteem measures to check on progress? How will you know that children are feeling more positive about themselves and their lives?

Some self-esteem scales can provide useful information upon which aspects of self-esteem a pupil needs support to be focused, for example, Pope, A. W. (1988) *The Five-scale Test of Self-esteem for Children: Junior and Secondary*.

Blasting the Blues Away!

When you feel 'down', how do you try to bring yourself out of it?

Share your ideas with a partner.

Activity Linked to Slide 10

Everyone feels low from time to time (when faced with disappointments or failure, for example). How do you avoid a long 'wallow'? What do you do to help yourself feel better?

Allow time for participants to discuss and then collate some of their responses on a flipcharts.

Self-esteem and Success

| People with low self-esteem | External attributions | 'The task was easy.' 'It was just luck.' |
| People with high self-esteem | Internal attributions | 'I persevered.' 'I worked really hard.' |

Facilitator Notes for Slide 11

People with low self-esteem find it hard to attribute success to any personal qualities. They're more likely to play down any achievement as being small or attribute it to chance. There is a tendency to view themselves as victims of circumstance rather than feeling empowered to determine their future.

If self-esteem is good, they can recognise their own abilities or acknowledge self-effort.

Self-esteem is about the judgement or opinion we hold of ourselves – the extent to which we perceive ourselves to be worthwhile and capable human beings.

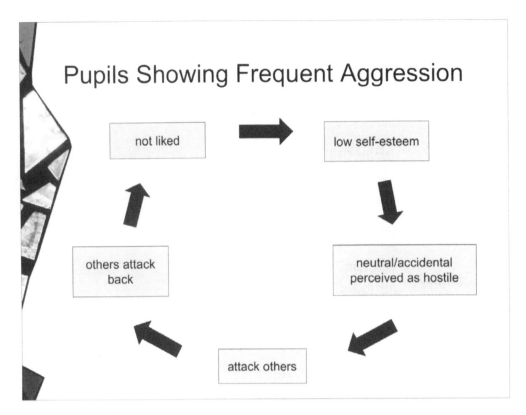

Facilitator Notes for Slide 12

Persistently aggressive children are caught in a negative cycle of feeling unworthy and unvalued. They are unpopular, which perpetuates their feelings of inadequacy. They tend to see everything through negative eyes, interpreting innocent actions or comments as threatening. They react with hostility, provoking hostile responses from others. This in turn confirms and reinforces their feelings of being disliked.

Perhaps if we can break into this cycle by supporting them to raise their self-esteem and at the same time become more skilled at seeing things from other people's points of view, we may be able to help them reduce their aggression and enter into more productive relationships.

Characteristics of High and Low Self-esteem

- On Day 1 you identified some characteristics you thought matched high and low self-esteem.

- What can we do to help children move in the right direction – from low self-esteem towards high self-esteem?

Facilitator Notes for Slide 13

Pin up the flipchart responses from Day 1 or if they have been typed up give them out.

This slide is not an activity in itself – it links to the following section of the presentation.

In order to answer this question, it will help if we can focus on specific aspects of self-esteem.

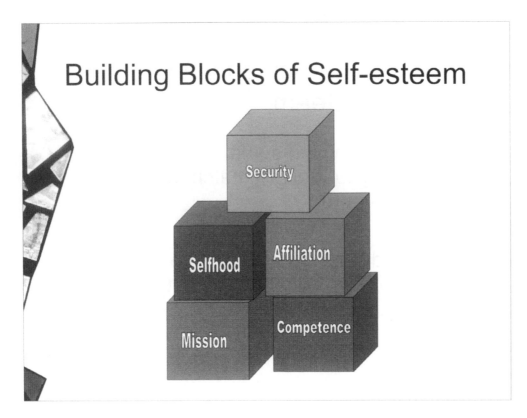

Building Blocks of Self-esteem

Michelle Borba's work on self-esteem recognises five distinct areas that contribute to a person's self-esteem. These building blocks should be seen as sequential, so in this illustration we need to start at the top and work down. (Borba, M. (1989) Esteem Builders' Complete Programme.)

1. Security is about feeling safe and at ease. Being able to trust others.

2. Selfhood relates to self-awareness – knowing the sort of things that make you 'you'. It relates to physical characteristics as well as personality factors and knowing and understanding your own feelings (emotional literacy).

3. Affiliation refers to a sense of belonging – knowing that others want us and need us; knowing that we matter.

4. Mission is about motivation – having a sense of purpose in our lives, feeling empowered to make choices, being able to look ahead, being able to take responsibility.

5. Competence relates to awareness about our own abilities – being realistic about our achievements and able to accept our limitations. It includes the realisation that we're not stuck with what we have now – we have the ability to develop new skills.

Borba provides a model which identifies the component parts of self-esteem (rather than treating it as a very broad general concept) which enables a much more closely targeted focus and support for development.

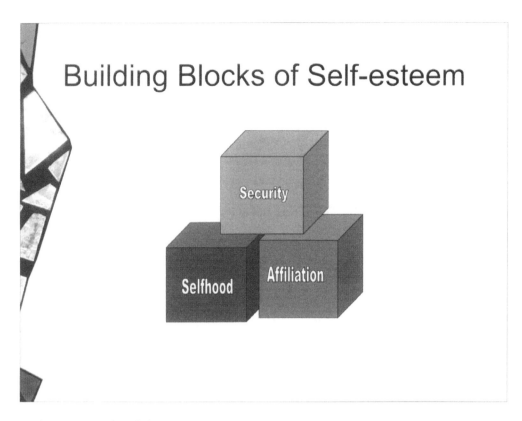

Building Blocks of Self-esteem

Facilitator Notes for Slide 15

When we focus on trying to raise self-esteem we often go in at too high a level. If self-esteem in these first three areas is not strong then work on mission and competence is unlikely to be effective.

These first three building blocks are the areas that we are most likely to need to focus on in a pupil with low self-esteem, so the remainder of the presentation will focus on these three aspects.

Only when we are sure that a pupil is secure, aware of their personal attributes and feel they belong should we try to work directly on their level of motivation or sense of competence. These latter two might in any case be most influenced by the general school ethos of teaching and learning.

Security

A pupil with a high measure on security:

- feels safe
- knows there are people he/she can count on
- can trust and depend on the teacher, LSA, key adult
- can handle change or spontaneity without undue discomfort
- comprehends the roles and limits expected in situations.

Facilitator Notes for Slide 16

We will start by looking more closely at the first of the foundational building blocks – security:

- A high level of security conveys a strong sense of assuredness.
- It is essential for healthy emotional development.
- It is the foundation – a child must feel secure in their setting and be able to trust the adult who is attempting to enhance their self-esteem.

Security

Activity

1. If we put a 'does not' in front of the statements on the previous slide, what feelings might the pupil have?

2. What might we see or hear?

Share in whole group.

Activity Linked to Slide 17

In groups of three or four, discuss these two questions. Receive feedback as a whole group.

The signs of insecurity will include physiological stress/anxiety/fear – tense, nervous, showing extremes of emotion – angry outbursts, bursting into tears.

These children find it difficult to cope with new experiences because they are not very confident with what they already know. They consequently find change difficult because they perceive it as posing an even greater threat in an already challenging situation.

They are unsure about what is expected of them. Because they don't feel very safe they find it hard to trust others. They don't feel well looked after and they may therefore be trying to take an inappropriate amount of control over their own lives. They may try to build security by seeking to take control.

Esteem-builders to Security

- Build a trusting relationship.

- Activity
  - How do you think you could help an insecure child begin to trust you?

A child's trust has to be earned. It can take a great deal of time and care to move a child on in this area.

In the same small groups, discuss how we might get trust and security to a 'good enough' level?

Following discussion, collate examples on a flipchart.

Esteem-builders to Security

- Set reasonable limits and rules that are consistently enforced.

- Create a positive and caring environment.

Facilitator Notes for Slide 19

Letting children have too much of their own way doesn't increase their security. Discuss need for boundaries.

Being child-centred isn't about abdicating our responsibility to make key decisions in their lives; it's about being sensitive to their feelings and their needs. As they become more confident that we understand them and are responding supportively to their needs, they will find it easier to trust our judgements and respond to requests.

Giving restricted choices is a helpful transition, allowing the child to retain some legitimate control (for example, 'You can choose to do this activity first or that one. Which are you going to start with?').

It's important to be positive towards them – showing we like them and care about them. We need to help them feel special.

Building Self-esteem

- Sequential development.
- Security is a pre-requisite to other components.
- The core building blocks
  – security – self-hood – affiliation.
- From these foundations:
  mission – competence.

(Borba, 1989)

Facilitator Notes for Slide 20

Having looked in more detail at security, we are going to have a look at some key factors and how this model can help us with starting points for children.

Borba's model identifies security as an essential foundation.

And then, closely linked to this will be knowledge of self (selfhood), which is also an important building block for the sense of belonging (affiliation) – sequential development.

We are going to focus on these three, as these will be the areas where most of the children you will be working with will require support and appropriate targets.

Mission and competence are at higher levels of self-esteem.

Building Self-esteem

- Change takes place slowly.
- Consistency is critical.
- The environment and attitude of others, play a significant role.

(Borba, 1989)

Facilitator Notes for Slide 21

Change takes place slowly – this is important for us.

Our relationship, attitude and consistency really can make a difference.

We need to identify small stepped targets which may be context linked to show progress. We should not forget the importance of a child spontaneously initiating or responding with eye contact or a smile, if this rarely happens.

Your individual time with a child could well be the time when these developments first occur.

Building Blocks of Self-esteem

Activity (individual)

- Use the handout of positive descriptors for each of the first three building blocks of self-esteem.

- Consider and share information on two or three children you know/are working with in relation to these descriptors.

- Focus on the first three building blocks, and give a rating 1 (low) – 10 (high) for each of the pupils you have identified.

- From this, identify what you consider to be the priority aspect for focused development.

Activity Linked to Slide 22

Introduce the following handouts:

- Building Blocks of Self-esteem – Positive Descriptors.

- Building Blocks of Self-esteem – Rating Scales.

Participants should try to complete the rating scales for two or three children, and identify the priority focus. Leave the activities/interventions part for the moment.

Emphasise that within each building block there may be substantial areas to develop for particular individuals, from which a specific focus will need to be selected.

When they have done this activity – it will be useful to ask them to identify the 'can do' statements for their children. This can be a useful check on the size of the step from where the child is at and the focused target for development – and whether any adjustments need to be made!

Esteem-builders

Activity (in pairs)

- Use the handout – Practical Ideas and Activities to Support Sequential Development of Self-esteem – focus on selfhood.

- Share how you already use some of these ideas and how you might develop/use with specific pupils in your sessions.

Activity Linked to Slide 23

Introduce the following handout:

- Practical Ideas and Activities to Support Sequential Development of Self-esteem

Ask participants to include their ideas about emotional literacy – what activities, materials and so on, are they using or thinking about to take forward the language and understanding about emotions? Draw out things which will help them get started.

Esteem-builders

Activity (individual/small group)

- Go back to your own two or three pupils and complete the section 'What activities/interactions might help?'.
- Discuss and share in your group.

Activity Linked to Slide 24

Return to the following handout:

   • Building Blocks of Self-esteem – Rating Scales.

Now complete the section 'What activities/interactions might help?' Refer to the handout 'Practical Ideas and Activities to Support Sequential Development of Self-esteem' .

Allow time and encourage an exploration of the games and resources which are displayed, and a sharing of resources which participants have used or have knowledge of.

Longer-term Aim: To Enable Young People to Build Resilience

Establish the foundations:

- trust and security
- self knowledge – understanding and naming own emotions
- getting connectedness with others.

Provide opportunities to take steps towards:

- facing and coping with challenges
- feeling OK about making mistakes
- valuing challenge.

Facilitator Notes for Slide 25

We can help young people by how we support them:

- to take on small challenges

- recognise with them when they have been able to do things which were harder/a bit tricky, that didn't work out the first time but they stuck with them.

As these will often be exceptions for these children, we can help them to recognise their achievements, name their coping strategies, problem-solving, perseverance… which is part of helping them build resilience.

Give out handouts:

- Building Blocks of Self-esteem – A Focus on Developing Selfhood.
- Building Blocks of Self-esteem – A Focus on Developing Affiliation.

Building Blocks of Self-esteem – Positive Descriptors

Security

Pupil:

- can handle change or spontaneity without undue discomfort
- feels safe
- knows there are people he/she can count on
- can trust and depend on the teacher, LSA, key adult
- comprehends the roles and limits expected in situations.

A high level of security conveys a strong sense of assuredness.
It is essential for healthy emotional development.
It is the foundation – child must feel secure in their setting and be able to trust the adult who is attempting to enhance their self-esteem.

Selfhood

Pupil:

- has good sense of self-knowledge – accurate and realistic description of his roles, attributes and physical characteristics
- identifies and expresses emotions and attitude
- has a strong sense of individuality
- feels adequate and worthy of praise.

Affiliation

Pupil:

- feels good about their social experiences, generally feels connected to others and accepted
- has a sense of belonging – in a relationship – family, classmates, peers, friends
- is able to maintain friendships
- is able to co-operate and share and show compassion to others.

Friends have an enormous bearing on a pupil's feelings about who she is.

Day 2

Mission

Pupil:

- sets realistic and achievable goals
- can follow through on plans
- takes initiatives
- is responsible for her actions
- seeks alternatives to problems
- evaluates himself according to past performance
- is highly motivated
- is willing to take risks.

Pupil is aware of what she wants to achieve and goes through the process of getting there

Competence

Pupil:

- is aware of strengths and can accept weaknesses
- views mistakes as valuable learning tools.

Feelings of success must come from experiences that the individual sees as valuable and important. Feelings of being capable lead to a willingness to take risks, as well as to share opinions and ideas.

(Borba, 1989)

Jo Birbeck, Hampshire Educational Psychology Service

Building Blocks of Self-esteem – Rating Scales

Pupil's first name and initial of surname: ....

	low									high
Security	1	2	3	4	5	6	7	8	9	10
Selfhood	1	2	3	4	5	6	7	8	9	10
Affiliation	1	2	3	4	5	6	7	8	9	10

Priority focus:
What activities/interactions might help?

Jo Birbeck, Hampshire Educational Psychology Service.

Day 2

Practical Ideas and Activities to Support Sequential Development of Self-esteem

Building Blocks of Self-esteem

Where can we focus to help children begin to move from low self-esteem towards higher self-esteem?

Self-esteem building is sequential:

security   selfhood   affiliation (belonging)

and provides the core before moving to higher levels.

A Focus on Developing Security

What we might do to facilitate this:

Building trusting relationships - – role of key adults are:

- Time for personal recognition.
- Genuine interest – regular opportunities for interaction around their interests.
- Value the child and showing you like him.
- Recognise what she can do.
- Acknowledge and reward his achievements.
- Be reliable and consistent.
- LSA support in small groups.

Creating a positive and caring environment includes:

- 'Healthy school'.
- Build in bubble time, that is, start and end of day, time out, calming time.
- A gradual introduction to new situations – playtimes, dinner, assemblies.
- Buddy bench, game gangs.
- Structure playtimes with adult cover.
- Positive help and support for social skills, use social stories.

Having key rules and setting reasonable limits/boundaries:

- Key rules, consistently reinforced and rewarded.
- Establish structure, routines and patterns.
- On a daily basis, provide clear information – visual and short concise phrases.

'...You've got to help me. You've got to hold out your hand even when that's the last thing I seem to want or need.'

'...Each time you are kind and gentle and encouraging, each time you try to understand because you really care, my heart begins to grow wings, very small wings, very feeble wings, but wings.'

From 'Glad to be Me' edited by Don Peretz Elkins (1976).

Day 2

Building Blocks of Self-esteem
– A Focus on Developing Selfhood

What we might do to facilitate this:

- Recognise and value children's individuality.

- Help children to create individual positive books with photos, positive 'I' comments, descriptions, drawings, cut out pictures. Share and look at this on a regular basis.

- Name child's achievable goals – break down into 'bite size pieces', and the attributes they have to achieve them.

- Help child to recognise and name his achievements – encourage use of 'I' statements.

- Use specific praise, recognition and range of rewards, for example, awards, certificates, displaying work.

- Name and give praise for strategies they use at difficult times, for example, praise for calming down.

- Build in a range of self-awareness and expression exercises as attention breaks in the curriculum.

- Provide opportunities and value children's choices.

- Develop 'emotional literacy' – range of language about emotions linked to their experiences and stories, bring into day to day activities/events – name, check out and acknowledge their feelings/moods – show you understand things from her perspective (empathy).

- Listen to children – bubble time.

- Build up a repertoire of positive statements which are used between adults and child/children, children to each other, building in time to promote this.

- Introduce strategies to refocus thinking to increase self-control in managing emotions, for example:

  o visualisation techniques such as 'putting your frazzles in your shoes'

  o visualise a positive place, time, event and actively recreate those positive feelings.

- Encourage role development: being a member of the school council, being a buddy/peer mentor; taking responsibility, for example, register, aspect of PE equipment/playtime equipment and so on; taking part in specific projects – writing/spelling; team building activities, for example, part of PE, residentials.

- Opportunities and focus in assemblies, Circle Time, PSHE.

Day 2

Building Blocks of Self-esteem
– A Focus on Developing Affiliation

What we might do to facilitate this.

Sense of belonging – promoting inclusion and acceptance (school, class, group):

- Encouragement to join clubs/interest groups – lunchtime, after school activities.
- Support whole-class or group identity – praise and reward system for whole class or group (cuddly toy, class points/smilies, sharing biscuits).
- Encourage responsibilities within the class/group or at school level – monitors, specific roles/responsibilities, school council.
- Topics about family, special days, valuing diversity in families.
- Help children to discover and share the interests, backgrounds, capabilities of each other, valuing similarities and differences.
- Enable each child in a group to participate and feel a part of the group.
- Golden time.
- Circle Time.
- VIP.

Co-operation, sharing, skills in friendship making:

- Visual cues for sharing, for example, picture to share crisps.
- Healthy snack time (across whole school) – children bring fruit which in class groups is pooled and cut up; a shared snack time is held each day.
- Encourage children to show approval to each other and give support, promote positive interactions/comments between children.
- Teach playground games to support co-operation and friendships.
- Structure games, explicitly promoting friendship and social skills.
- Friendship/buddy benches, game gang.
- Set up Circle of Friends.
- Lunchtime leaders – Year 5/6 'supervising' and supporting play of younger children.
- Progress awards for social and friendship skills.
- Bubble time.
- Structure co-operative group activities.

With thanks and acknowledgement to the Hampshire teacher co-ordinator and learning support assistant project participants:

Cupernham Infant School	Shepherds Spring Infant School	Norwood Primary School
Stoke Park Junior School	Scantabout Primary School	Weeke Primary School

Jo Birbeck, Hampshire Educational Psychology Service

Day 2

Slides 1-33

Active Listening and Communication Skills

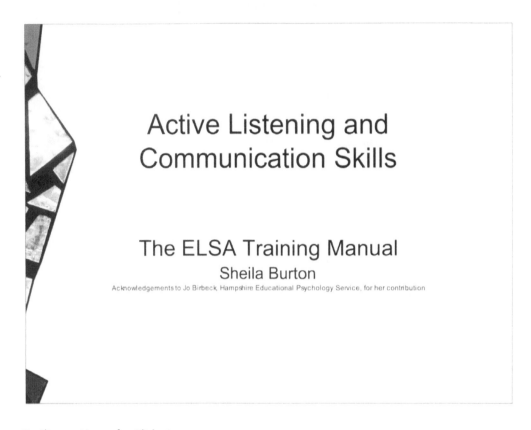

Active Listening and
Communication Skills

The ELSA Training Manual
Sheila Burton
Acknowledgements to Jo Birbeck, Hampshire Educational Psychology Service, for her contribution

Facilitator Notes for Slide 1

The facilitator will need to prepare the following resources for this session:

- Personal Observation and Reflection.

- Observation – Developing a Shared Understanding and Active   Listening Skills.

- Active Listening: Using Language to Help the Speaker.

Note: Do not give out copies of slide handout until session is complete. Slide 13 includes answers to the activity posed on the previous slide and pre-reading will spoil the activity.

Aims

- to have knowledge of elements of active listening and effective communication skills
- to consider these in:
  - building genuine relationships
  - enabling social and emotional development and learning
- to practice elements of active listening and effective communication
- to reflect on own strengths and growing points.

Facilitator Notes for Slide 2

In this session we will look at some of the key features of effective communication that help us to build good relationships, which are essential to supporting the development of the children and young people we work with.

We will notice the importance of how well we listen and there will be opportunity to practice active listening together so we can think about the skills we need to develop further.

Essentially Social

- We are essentially social beings.
- Why do we need to 'tune in', interpret from their perspective and 'really listen' to children?
- Successful communication and social interaction requires having space in your mind for the other person.

Facilitator Notes for Slide 3

Social communication is instinctive to us. This is evident even in newborn babies who enter into a kind of conversation with their parents and other attentive adults. They know how to take turns, synchronising their sounds and movements with the adult they are sharing attention with. This has been described as a kind of 'dance' between baby and parent.

Being listened to – active receiving (mirroring) is an essential human need from birth – it forms the foundation for core communication at any age. It is also the base upon which secure attachment is established.

Successful relationships form when people become attuned to each other.

Making a Difference in Children's Social and Emotional Development and Learning

- Security is a prerequisite to learning.
- Young people's life experiences are varied and result in differing and changing needs.
- Being understood and really 'listened to' continues to be an essential emotional and social need.
- Genuine and positive relationships make a difference.

Facilitator Notes for Slide 4

Feeling safe is one of our most basic human needs. Insecure children struggle to learn.

There will be times in children's lives when they need greater emotional support, especially at times of difficult change.

If they have people in their lives who are well-attuned to them, children will have greater resilience to cope with challenges.

Making a difference – we will explore the role of active listening skills, non-verbal and verbal, in our communication with young people. You will recognise the range of skills that you already have and maybe identify one or two things that you would like to check out, do more of or perhaps plan to develop.

Some Barriers to Communication in a Helping Relationship

- Judging – being critical of the child.
- Avoiding child's concerns by:
  - diverting the conversation
  - imposing logical argument
  - reassuring prematurely.
- Sending solutions – telling the child what to do about a problem.

Facilitator Notes for Slide 5

We are briefly going to consider some barriers which can occur in a helping relationship before we focus on the helpful values and skills which will be the main focus of this session:

Judging

Be careful not to imply criticism in the way you respond to children. Avoid reinforcing their sense of inadequacy or failure. Show understanding of their difficulties.

Avoiding the Child's Concerns

This is sometimes done by taking the conversation off in a different direction. Other times we use logic to argue against a child's worries.

If we try to reassure the child before they have really been able to air their concerns they will not be able to receive our attempted reassurance. They will more likely feel we're not taking account of their feelings seriously.

Sending Solutions

Working in education we develop areas of expertise, but resist the temptation to be the 'expert'. Children may have significant insight into their own difficulties. Avoid pushing them into solutions they are not comfortable with. Help them choose their own.

If we take the role of a facilitator rather than an instructor children will respond better to our intervention. Validate their own ideas where possible. We all respond better to encouragement than criticism.

Building a Positive Relationship

Key aspects for starting to establish security and build a supportive relationship:

- Respect.
- Genuineness.
- Empathy.

Facilitator Notes for Slide 6

It is important to recognise that in a one-to-one session, you can give the attention and time to 'really' listen to the child, often in a way that is not possible in the class or wider group situations. This enables us to try to avoid some of the barriers which may arise – we will be looking at ways which can help us later in today's session. First of all we are going to focus on the importance of building a positive relationship.

We're going to look at three important features of a supportive relationship:

1. Respect.

2. Genuineness.

3. Empathy.

We'll take each one in turn and think about what it means in the context of working with a child.

Respect

A respectful attitude to children includes:

- caring about their wellbeing
- feeling they are worth your time and effort
- regarding each one as unique
- assuming the goodwill of the child
- maintaining confidentiality.

Facilitator Notes for Slide 7

Respect means valuing others simply because they are human beings. You don't have to approve of everything they do, but you need to respect their intrinsic value as a person.

Respect is shown both in your attitude towards children and in the way you work with them.

Your attitude towards children is respectful if you:

- care about the wellbeing of the child

- feel that 'working with this child is worth my time and effort'

- regard each child as unique and take the time to value the child for who he/she is and what he/she brings to the relationship

- assume the child is 'good at heart' (remember – they don't intend to be a problem, but are trying in their own ways to resolve the problems they perceive)

- maintain their confidentiality (within the accepted limits) – don't tell other people things that the child only wanted to share with you, unless you perceive the child to be at risk of harm or to be endangering others.

Genuineness

You are genuine when you:

- are interested in the child and do not over-emphasise your professional role
- are spontaneous but not uncontrolled
- remain open and non-defensive (even when threatened)
- are consistent between your values and behaviour
- are open about yourself.

Facilitator Notes for Slide 8

Genuineness means being at ease with yourself and not having to play a 'role' when talking with others.

You are genuine in your relationships with children when:

- you don't over-emphasise your professional role and you avoid stereotyped role behaviour – be yourself, don't try to be a different kind of person when you talk with a child

- you are able to be spontaneous in your responses to them but not uncontrolled (if they're upset it won't help for you to burst into tears too!)

- you don't change your positive attitude towards them even when they are being difficult (continue to like them even when you dislike the behaviour)

- you are consistent between your own values and behaviour – whilst remaining tactful and respectful towards the child who may not share your values

- you are open – willing to share some of your own experiences (within reason!).

Empathy

Communicating to children that you understand their:

- experiences
- behaviours
- feelings.

Seeing things from their perspective.

Facilitator Notes for Slide 9

Empathy is about communicating understanding – being able to relate to the child's feelings.

It is being able to see things from their perspective – 'stepping into their shoes'.

We can show empathy by how well we listen and interpret, from verbal and non-verbal communication, what it is like from the child's perspective at that time. This includes the feelings and 'hidden' messages behind their behaviour.

Empathy can involve reflecting back what the child is saying/communicating, and we will look at this in more detail a little later – restating and reflecting feelings.

Empathy promotes the sense of 'belonging'.

Borba's model of self esteem (1989)

Maslow's hierarchy of needs (1987).

Attending and Non-attending – Why are Feelings Important?

- Activity (in pairs)
  Talking and not listening – not attending!
  Do this for one minute and then reverse roles.
- Reflect on:
  - the feelings you had as the speaker
  - what happens when we do not feel we are being listened to
  - how our behaviour changes.
- What would you do differently?

Activity Linked to Slide 10

Work in pairs. One person takes the role of speaker. The other is actively **not** listening (looking elsewhere, fidgeting, doing other things). Time for one minute then tell everyone to swap roles. Time for one more minute. Reflect in pairs and then share in whole group.

Can participants think of examples when they have not been listened to? Partners, own children, times at work?

This activity gives the opportunity to draw out how some people shut down and withdraw while others become angry and frustrated. Our feelings will reflect whether we feel valued and will very much affect how we communicate, and how we feel about ourselves.

What would you do differently? This question provides the opportunity to detail the importance of giving attention and what this looks like, that is, with our bodies, facial expressions, mirroring and so on. Also the importance of synchrony with the speaker's message – movements, eye contact/glances – the foundations of good communication at any level.

Attending and Actively Receiving

- Do you listen carefully to what the child says and what their body language is conveying, or are you rehearsing your reply?
- Do you listen carefully to the child's point of view, even when you sense this point of view needs to be challenged?
- Are you aware of your biases and how they affect your ability to listen?
- Are you aware of what distracts you from listening carefully and what you can do to manage those distractions?

Facilitator Notes for Slide 11

There's always a danger that we don't listen fully to what a child is telling us because we've predicted what their message is about and are planning our response, especially since children can be rather long-winded in their explanations and we tend to be very conscious of time.

Sometimes we are too quick to correct what we see as faulty thinking or inaccuracy on the part of the child.

We all have biases or prejudices that can affect our listening. We may take the child less seriously or jump to false conclusions as a result of our own biased thinking.

We often talk about distractible children, but how aware are we of our own distractibility? How can we help ourselves to be more focused?

Activity Linked to Slide 11

Ask participants to read through the bullet points in this slide and share their thinking with a partner – can they recognise when they may do some of these? (There is no need to collect feedback.)

Communication Consists Of:

1. using our body –
   posture, movements,
   facial expressions
2. using paralanguage –
   voice tone, inflection,
   pace, speed of speech
3. using the spoken word
   Activity (in pairs):
   - what percentage do you
     think each of these three
     components accounts
     for?

Day 2

Facilitator Notes for Slide 12

There are three recognised elements to communication:

1. Body language.

2. Paralanguage.

3. Spoken language.

Activity Linked to Slide 12

Ask participants to jot down, on their own, their estimates of the percentage contribution of each (which should total 100%). Take some feedback.

Answers are on the next slide.

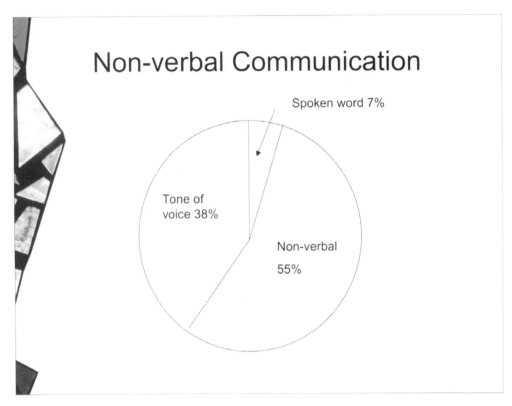

Non-verbal Communication

Spoken word 7%

Tone of voice 38%

Non-verbal 55%

Facilitator Notes for Slide 13

Using our body (non-verbal signals).   55%

Using paralanguage (tone, speed, inflection etc.).   38%

Using the spoken word.   7%

(These figures are taken from Conciliation Skills, SCRIP 2002.)

Make links with the previous activities and the power of the communication in using our body and paralanguage (non-verbal communication).

This will link with an activity on Day 4 – the different meanings from one sentence depending on the 'paralanguage'.

Non-verbal Communication

Be aware of child's:	Be aware of *your:*
• posture and movements	• posture and movements
• facial expression	• facial expression
• tone of voice.	• tone of voice.

These will tell you how the child is feeling.

These will tell the child how *you* are feeling.

Facilitator Notes for Slide 14

We need to be attentive not just to what a child is saying but to their whole demeanour, and pick up on any contradictions between what they say and what their bodies are saying (the non-verbal communication will reflect the 'real' feelings if there is a contradiction with what is being said).

This applies to us as well as to the children. We need to ensure that our non-verbal signals are not contradicting what we're saying – otherwise the child will disbelieve us. Children are very good at seeing through us if we're just pretending to be positive.

Active Listening

'Active "whole body" listening means being able to give all of your attention to someone else. It is the ability to keep your attention external to yourself rather than thinking through your own thoughts.'

(Conciliation Skills, SCRIP, 2002.)

Facilitator Notes for Slide 15

This quote can be linked back to 'having space in your mind for the other person'.

Listening is not a passive process. We need to work hard at really listening to what a child is saying. How well we listen will have a considerable impact on the quality of their 'sharing'.

Active Listening Involves:

Attending and receiving – giving active attention to the non-verbal communication, the feelings of the person and what they say by:

- attentive whole-body and facial expressions
- making encouraging sounds, repeating key words or short phrases
- taking short turns, pauses, slowing the pace
- attuned mirroring – 'like a dance'.

Facilitator Notes for Slide 16

This draws together the non-verbal communication covered so far and again emphasises the synchrony between the adult and child – how the adult is 'tuning in' to the child and their feelings and actively supporting the communication through their focused attention.

Active Listening Involves:

- Checking out our understanding and facilitating their reflection by:
  - clarifying, restating
  - reflecting back the other person's feelings
  - summarising.
- Facilitating their understanding and thinking, and identifying their own possible ways forward by:
  - asking open, reflective questions.

Facilitator Notes for Slide 17

We are now going to look in more detail at using language in active listening skills.

Clarifying

Some examples:

- 'Can you tell me more about that?'
- 'Do you mean…?'
- 'Is this the problem as you see it now?'

Facilitator Notes for Slide 18

Clarifying involves questions, which can be open or closed. What is the difference?

Why Clarify?

- To get additional information to help us understand clearly
- To help exploration of different aspects.

Facilitator Notes for Slide 19

We clarify to be sure we understand correctly the message the child is trying to convey to us.

Restating

This often paraphrases an important piece of
information or key aspects of what has been
communicated to you (reflecting back), for example:
- 'From what you are saying, I understand that...'
- '...is important to you.'
- 'You have decided to... and the reasons are...'

Facilitator Notes for Slide 20

Restating provides the opportunity for making a statement (not a question) and pausing. This allows the child to take things further or not – it is less intrusive than questions and gives control to the child in relation to the direction.

Links with empathy in relation to what is being said. It's your way of saying, 'I'm with you. I've been listening carefully to what you've been saying and I'm checking to make sure I understand.'

Why Restate?

- To show you have listened and received.
- To check out your understanding.
- To slow the pace and encourage thinking.
- To encourage exploration of a different or other aspect of the issues being discussed.

Facilitator Notes for Slide 21

It allows 'thinking' time by encouraging a slower pace.

It values and gives importance to the child and helps them to explore at a deeper level to increase understanding.

It enables a greater level of 'attunement' with the young person – as well as non-verbal synchrony, there is verbal synchrony with mirroring and checking out. With appropriate pausing after restating, we can create the 'space' for more reflective thinking from the young person we are helping.

Try to notice how often you use restating or reflecting back as part of your normal conversational style.

Receiving and Reflecting Feelings

- Feelings underlie motivation, interest, behaviour and learning in any situation.

- They are an essential part of the knowledge, understanding and reflection about ourselves – a core component in the foundations of self-esteem (Borba, 1989).

Facilitator Notes for Slide 22

Draw out the importance of 'emotional literacy' (understanding the link between feelings and behaviour) which applies to children and adults alike.

Our knowledge of ourselves, the understanding and expression of our feelings and their regulation are a key component within self-esteem which links with self-empowerment. (The building blocks of self-esteem: security, selfhood, affiliation, mission, competence, Borba, 1989.)

Reflecting Feelings

Some examples:

- 'It looks as if this is feeling a bit tricky – it's sometimes hard to think up ideas when you have to write.'
- 'Getting a certificate in assembly made you feel really proud of yourself.'
- 'You are feeling quite frustrated because Jade doesn't want to play the game the same way as you.'

Facilitator Notes for Slide 23

Link this to the earlier slide on empathy.

This is about listening to the whole message, that is, the feelings behind or underneath the behaviour – what you see or hear.

Why Reflect Feelings?

- To **actively receive** and show that we are giving our attention to things important to them.
- To **name what we are interpreting** from their verbal and non-verbal communication.
- To **check out** that we are interpreting accurately.
- To **help them recognise and give time to their emotions,** and to develop and express their understanding.

Remember, reflect back feelings and pause – hand the turn back.

Facilitator Notes for Slide 24

Reflecting feelings enables us to help a child who may not be fully aware of their emotions or have the language to describe them. We tentatively name these and check out with them. This in its own right actively supports the development of emotional literacy through the opportunities that arise when working with children, as well as being incorporated into our one-to-one work with individual children.

It is important to find and practise phrases that we feel comfortable with, when this is something we want to develop or increase in our own skills.

Reflecting Positive Feelings

Jonathan has been building a model of a windmill. The blades kept getting stuck. He has tried out different ways to change his construction. He is smiling as he spins and watches the blades go around…

Activity (in pairs).
What might the adult say to reflect back the positive feelings?

Facilitator Notes for Slide 25

When thinking about reflecting back feelings, it can be helpful to develop our skills, starting with reflecting back positive feelings with children. Adult comment could be, 'What a lovely smile Jonathan. It looks as if you are feeling pleased with your model,' or, 'It looks as if you're pleased with what you have done.'

This is a very good opportunity to draw out the difference between giving praise and reflecting back feelings. You are likely to find that participants tend to focus on the behaviours rather than the feelings and attention can be drawn to this when receiving examples from the activity.

Praise: giving approval, power resides with the adult, can relate to the adult's needs in relation to the child, is quicker, can be given when our attention is shared, can be given in different ways.

Reflecting feelings: attunement - adult is in the moment with the child, shares the pleasure through reflective (mirroring) response, names what they see, names the emotion for the child (emotional literacy) – it is the attunement in the relationship which is 'rewarding' for the child – empowering, requires focused attention, interest and time.

Both praise and reflecting feelings are important – they reflect different dynamics and support different aspects of development.

Activity Linked to Slide 25

In pairs, participants should think about ways of reflecting back Jonathan's feelings to him (that is, naming the feelings).

Examples of Open Reflective Questions

- How do you feel about…?
- What do you think about…?
- What happened to make you feel cross?
- Is there anything else that you could have done?
- If you could do it over again, how would you handle it differently?
- What might be the effect of that?

Facilitator Notes for Slide 26

Here are a few examples of open, reflective questions. They encourage the young person to think in greater depth about situations.

Why Use Open Reflective Questions?

- To give time to think about different aspects of the situation/problem.
- To enable expression of underlying or explicit feelings.
- To explore understanding and how feelings might affect the situation.
- Later, to explore possible ways forward.
- To empower and prevent 'rushing into' finding solutions for someone.

Facilitator Notes for Slide 27

Open, reflective questions are designed to help children and young people explore the impact of their feelings. We cannot assume that they are aware of the link between their feelings and their behaviour. These questions give them the space to explore their experiences with a helping adult.

Facilitating a Conversation

Activity (in groups of three).

Consider non-verbal skills, restating, reflecting feelings, open reflective questions:

- talker/problem owner, listener/communication partner, observer roles
- listener to facilitate the problem owner to talk about an identified work-related issue – four minutes
- observer completes sheet, is timer and facilitates the feedback
- rotate roles.

Facilitator Notes for Slide 28

This is the opportunity for participants to practise some of the skills that have been talked about.

Activity Linked to Slide 28

Allow at least 30 minutes for this activity – five minutes each to facilitate a conversation plus five minutes feedback for each facilitator following their turn.

Client to choose a 'safe' work-related issue which they are comfortable to talk about, that is, not something which is very personal and emotional.

Observer uses activity page, Observation – Developing a Shared Understanding and Active Listening Skills.

Note examples of these skills being used.

Observer facilitating feedback – see next slide.

Observer Role

Observer facilitates sharing of information and reflection by asking:

- adult 1 (listener/communication partner)
  - How did you feel?
  - What did you do that you are pleased with?
- adult 2 (talker/problem owner)
  - How did you know you were being listened to?
  - Was there anything else the listener did which you liked?

Observer feedback to listener/communication partner – adds in positive comments from Observation.

Activity Linked to Slide 29

The observer has a key role in asking the two participants in the role-play to reflect on how they experienced it.

Individual Reflection

- Reflect on and summarise the skills you often use in your listening and communication with children in your day-to-day work.

- Identify what you would like to check out or do more of.

Activity Linked to Slide 30

Draw attention to the activity page, Personal Observation and Reflection.

After everyone has taken a turn as the listener in this activity, a few minutes could be allowed for participants to fill in their personal reflection sheet, identifying skills they know they often use and those they would like to develop further (growing points).

Ending your Individual Session

- Summarise the main points of the discussion, especially agreed actions, for example, 'Today, we have talked about...'
- Encourage the child to talk further in the future – let them know you are accessible.
- End on a positive – reiterate the child's qualities/strengths.
- Thank the child for talking with you – be appreciative of their interest.

Facilitator Notes for Slide 31

This slide is about how to end an ELSA session.

When you come towards the end of a session with a child, it's helpful to summarise the main points that have been covered.

Let the child know you look forward to seeing them again. Let them know they can seek you out before any planned session if they need to talk to you.

Make sure you end your time together on a positive note. You want them to feel good when they leave you. Give them encouragement.

Don't forget to thank them for working with you.

Active Listening in a Genuine Relationship

Enables a young person to:
- be valued for who they are
- begin to feel secure
- initiate and sustain appropriate social interaction and communication
- have shared times and enjoyment.

Facilitator Notes Linked to Slide 32

These last two slides summarise the importance of active listening in empowering children and young people to value themselves and make positive choices.

Active Listening in a Genuine Relationship

Enables a young person to:

- be able to consider suggestions and make choices

- receive guidance and help

- begin to be aware of others – to be helped to wait, take turns…

- begin to be part of problem-solving when conflict/difficulties arise.

Observation – Developing a Shared Understanding and Active Listening Skills

Attending and encouraging: • to help the speaker express his/her thoughts and feelings and later find possible ways forward.	Observations:
With our body: • looking towards • facing/turning towards • open, relaxed body posture • facial expressions • body movements/nodding.	
With our para-language: • voice tone, pitch, inflection • speed of speech • pace – waiting/pausing • encouraging sounds (mm, uh-huh).	
With our language: • actively receiving – repeating key words/short phrases • clarifying • restating/paraphrasing • open reflective questions • reflecting feelings • summarising.	
Additional notes:	
Name:	Observation by:

Jo Birbeck
Hampshire Educational Psychology Service

Day 2

Personal Observation and Reflection

Strengths and Growing Points

What do I do in my daily work with children?	
Comments	Context – if relevant
I usually…	
I would like to check out…	
I would like to do more of/try out…	
How well did it go?	
What next?	

Day 2

Active Listening: Using Language to Help the Speaker

Attending and encouraging: to help the speaker explore and express his/her thoughts and feelings, and later find ways forward

Type	Purpose	Examples
Neutral receiving/encouraging	• to convey that you are interested and listening • to encourage the person to continue talking.	• Repeating short phrases they use, for example, 'two main things'. • 'I see.' • 'Uh-huh.' • 'That's very interesting.' • 'I understand.'
Open reflective questions	• to help her express and understand feelings • to give time to think about different aspects of a problem • later, to explore possible ways forward.	• 'How do you feel about...?' • 'What do you think about...?' • 'What did you like about that?' • 'What happened to make you feel cross?'
Clarifying	• to get at additional facts • to help her explore all sides of a problem.	• 'Can you clarify this?' • 'Do you mean this...?' • 'Is this the problem as you see it now?'
Paraphrasing/restating	• to check our meaning and interpretation • to show you are listening and that you understand what he/she is saying • to encourage him to analyse other aspects of matter being considered and to discuss it with you.	• 'As I understand it, ...' • 'You have decided to do... and the reasons are...'
Reflecting feelings	• to show that you understand how he/she feels about what he/she is saying • to help the person to evaluate and temper his/her own feelings as expressed by someone else.	• 'You feel that...' • 'It sounds as if you were quite shocked by what you saw' • 'You felt you didn't get a fair show'
Summarising	• to bring all the discussions into focus in terms of a summary • to serve as a springboard for further discussion on a new aspect or problem.	• 'These are the key ideas you have expressed...' • 'If I understand how you feel about the situation...'

Jo Birbeck, Hampshire Educational Psychology Service

Day 3

Content and Plan

PowerPoint Presentation – Understanding and Managing Anger (slides and notes)

Working with Puppets (DVD) and Facilitator Notes

Supporting Documents:

1. The Firework Model – an activity page for analysing an angry incident
   (Linked to Slide 7)

2. Managing Anger at Different Stages of the Assault Cycle
   (Linked to slides 11-17)

3. Planning an Anger Management Programme – Outline of Session Plans

4. Anger Management – Lessons from the Animal kingdom

5. Communicating through Puppets – Key Stages 1/2

6. Communicating through Puppets – Key Stages 2/3

Day 3

Content and Plan

The primary focus of the third training day is anger management. Before trying to manage anger it is important to have a clear understanding of the nature of this emotion. The training module considers the physiological changes that accompany it and presents a useful model – the firework model – for analysing the stages of an angry reaction. This has been found to be an effective model for helping children and young people reflect on their angry feelings. There is often a tendency for adults to want to tell children about calming strategies without first helping them to reflect on what is happening for them. This module provides a more comprehensive structure for anger management work by suggesting a progressive programme that first of all recognises the normality of the emotion and its potential benefits. It is not about eradicating angry feelings, but learning to recognise why they are occurring and then learning to reduce any negative impact for self and for others. A key area is making the link between thoughts, feelings and behaviour, learning how thoughts can power up or depower angry feelings.

There is also a module on Day 3 about the value of using puppets in work with children and young people of all ages. A DVD is provided of a training session delivered to ELSAs by the author. This includes explanation of the purpose behind using puppets and various ideas for how to use them. A demonstration of a therapeutic approach involving an adult client is included as an example of how puppets may be used to enrich conversations. By modeling the value of puppets in adult work ELSAs are enabled to consider how they might incorporate them in work with teenagers. This module is included alongside anger management because anger is an area of work that lends itself to a particular way of using animal puppets.

Essential reading: Chapter 5 of the course handbook (Shotton and Burton, 2008).

Suggested timings for the day:

9.15   Review of progress.

9.45   Presentation: Understanding and Managing Anger – slides 1-10.

10.45   Tea/coffee.

11.15   Presentation: Understanding and Managing Anger – slides 11-20.

12.15   Lunch.

1.00   Presentation by DVD: Working with Puppets.

1.45   Discussion of puppet DVD.

2.00   Planning some anger management sessions (in groups).

3.00   Plenary.

3.15   End.

Slides 1-20

Understanding and Managing Anger

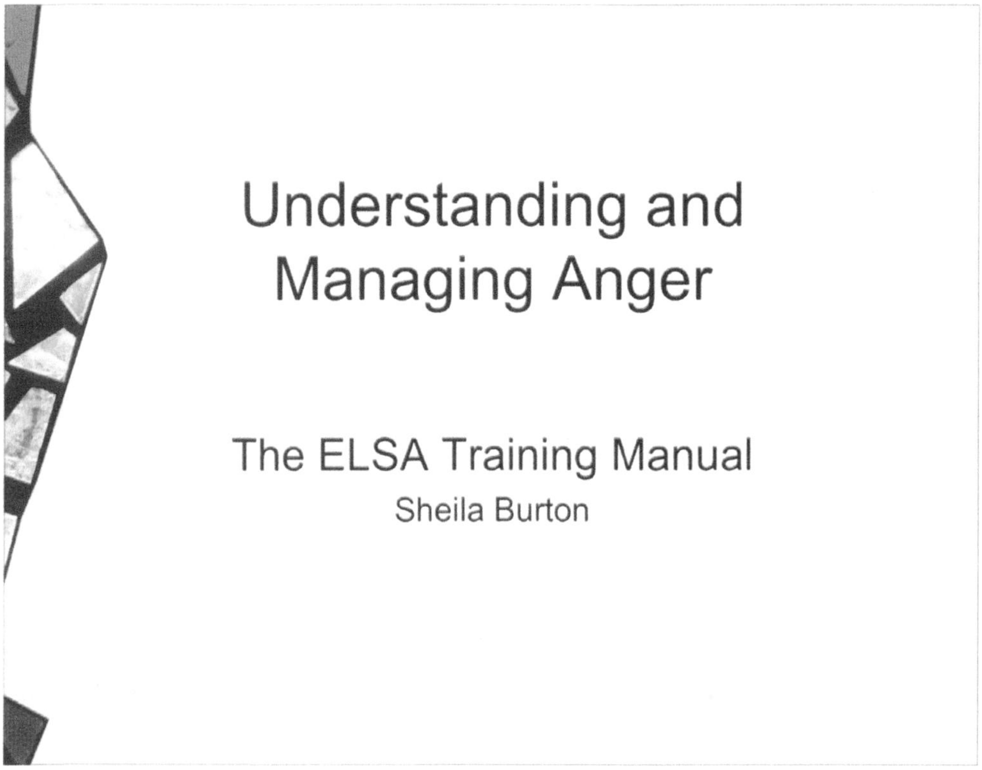
Understanding and
Managing Anger
The ELSA Training Manual
Sheila Burton

Facilitator Notes for Slide 1

This training module seeks to broaden trainees' understanding of anger. This will inform effective management of a powerful emotion which, unchecked, can have devastating consequences for our wellbeing.

A key recommended resource is Anger Management: A Practical Guide (1998) by Faupel, Herrick and & Sharp. This book explores the nature of anger and strategies for managing it effectively. It also incorporates some useful activity pages for work with children and young people.

Also useful is A Volcano in My Tummy (1996) by Whitehouse and Pudney which provides a possible intervention programme.

You will need to prepare the handout, Managing Anger at Different Stages of the Assault Cycle for this session.

Aims

The aims are to:

- understand the nature of anger
- explore effective anger management
- highlight key elements of an intervention programme.

Facilitator Notes for Slide 2

This training will raise awareness about the relationship of anger to other emotions. It will consider its purpose and the different ways in which it may be expressed. A useful conceptual model will be presented that helps to explain the key components of an angry response.

The biological basis of anger will be acknowledged, providing a key to its effective management, particularly with respect to the timing and nature of intervention. A variety of possible calming strategies will be suggested.

Important elements of an anger management programme will be discussed, giving a balanced intervention structure that can be tailored to individual needs.

What is Anger?

- Fierce displeasure; strong and passionate emotion excited by a sense of wrong.
- A secondary emotion arising from another primary emotion.
  For example, fear, embarrassment, disappointment, frustration, sorrow.
- A normal human emotion (with potential benefits).
- What does it look like?
  Think of as many words as possible that might link to anger.

Facilitator Notes for Slide 3

Cassell's Concise English dictionary definition incorporates these aspects. Attention needs to be drawn to other features – it can vary in intensity from relatively mild and transient annoyance to extreme and explosive fury. It tends to be an instinctive reaction rather than a rational response. When anger is aroused we are not always able to explain or even understand the underlying reasons for our angry feelings at the time.

It can be argued that anger does not appear as an isolated emotion, but will always be associated with at least one other emotion that constitutes some kind of threat to our sense of wellbeing. Trainees could be asked to think of times when they or someone they know has displayed anger as a result of any one of these other emotions.

It is important to emphasise the normality of anger. It is often perceived as something to be avoided, yet it can be a trigger for positive change. It is possible to think of examples at a political level, such as Wilberforce's lifelong work towards the abolition of slavery. Another might be the ending of child labour, bringing to a close the practice of committing young children to long days of hard manual work down coalmines or up chimneys. These changes were promoted by people who were acutely aware of and undoubtedly angered by the injustice of social practices at those times. At a personal level anger may motivate some to extricate themselves from abusive relationships, or to fight for an expensive medical treatment that might save the life of a loved one. If we never experienced anger we would not be fully human. The aim is not to eradicate anger but to be able to exercise some control over it, rather than allowing ourselves to be controlled by it.

Activity Linked to Slide 3

Before showing next slide, ask participants to brainstorm as many words as they can think of related to how anger might look. Note them on a flipchart.

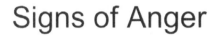

Signs of Anger

1. **Physical changes** – for example, heart rate, facial colour, muscle tension, sweating.

2. **Emotional feeling** – for example, irritability, tearfulness, stress/frustration.

3. **Behaviours** – for example, shouting, hitting, kicking, sulking, withdrawing.

Facilitator Notes for Slide 4

1. Anger gives rise to physical changes as a result of chemicals released into the bloodstream. For example, adrenalin increases heart rate and glucose fuels the muscles. Slide 12 which shows the assault cycle will also reflect chemical influence. The physical changes can be useful early warning indicators, both to the angry person and to others.

2. Irritability, tearfulness, frustration and other emotional indicators may accompany anger.

3. There is a range of possible behaviours that might arise from anger, some of which could be described as 'acting out' and others as 'acting in' behaviours.

The words noted on the flipchart from the activity on the previous slide could now be linked (for example, by colour coding) to these three categories.

Activity Linked to Slide 4

It may be appropriate to ask trainees to reflect upon their own styles of anger expression, including physiological indicators. They could be asked to think about the last time they remember feeling angry and recall how they showed it and how they resolved it.

Frequent Anger

- Frequently expressed anger indicates underlying emotional difficulties.
- Potential long-term effects:
  - mental health difficulties
  - family and friendship difficulties
  - violence towards self/others
  - conflict with law.

Facilitator Notes for Slide 5

Where anger is a way of life we need to be aware of any underlying emotional difficulties in order to provide appropriate support. It also enables us to contextualise rather than criticise the behaviour.

Where issues are not addressed there are likely to be serious long-term consequences:

- There will, at the very least, be serious self-esteem issues.

- Relationships will be adversely affected.

- Those who externalise their anger tend to be aggressive towards others and at risk of committing an offence, while those who internalise their anger are more likely to be caught up in self-harming behaviours.

- Examples of extreme road rage hit the news from time to time. A large percentage of murders are domestic offences. There have been many incidents of fatal youth stabbings in conflict situations.

The Anger Challenge

'Anyone can become angry – that is easy.
But to be angry with the right person, to
the right degree, at the right time, for the
right purpose, and in the right way – this
is not easy.'

(Aristotle, quoted by Goleman, 1995)

Facilitator Notes for Slide 6

In his book Emotional Intelligence Daniel Goleman includes this wonderful quote from the Ancient Greek philosopher Aristotle.

It is easy to find examples from our everyday lives of getting it wrong. Imagine a day when everything seems to go wrong:

- A traffic jam makes you late for work.

- The teacher's ill and you have to manage the class until a supply teacher arrives, but the pupils play up.

- You're also on playground duty that day and spend most of your time sorting out squabbles.

- You have to stay behind after school to complete an incident log following a classroom fight.

- When you get home your teenage son complains about you being late because he needs tea early tonight.

- You explode, telling him he's the laziest, most inconsiderate member of the family! A row ensues and he storms off in a temper.

Ask participants if they can supply any examples of their own.

The challenge is to become more aware of our own emotional state, as well as other people's emotional states and the impact we have on them.

This is lifelong learning. We need to remember that children have had fewer years to learn and not expect more than is reasonable from them. It's helpful to ask ourselves what their anger is communicating and reflect this back to them, so they eventually learn to verbalise their feelings for themselves.

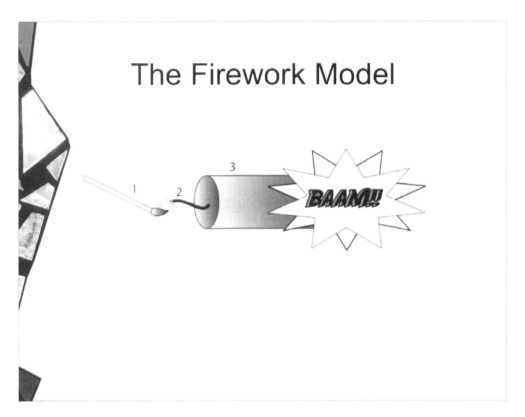

The Firework Model

Facilitator Notes for Slide 7

This visual model has proved very helpful in explaining anger arousal to children and young people. It provides an accessible way for them to analyse angry outbursts with a supporting adult. It is helpful to at least use an illustration of the model, and better still a three dimensional model. Children would enjoy making this as part of an anger management programme and this would help to strengthen their understanding and memory of the model.

The Firework Model

Useful three part model for describing angry outbursts:

1. Trigger – the match that lights the fuse.
2. Fuse – the thoughts and feelings set off by the trigger situation or event.
3. The firework body – physiological changes produced by thoughts and feelings can lead to explosive behaviour.

Facilitator Notes for Slide 8

The model recognises that angry reactions are triggered by a situation or event (a trigger).

It is our emotional and cognitive responses to the situation or event that power up the anger (the fuse). These are a reflection of our personal perceptions of the trigger – the meaning we give to what is happening. (And we can also learn to use cognitive processes to defuse our angry reactions, which is the purpose of anger management programmes.)

Sensory information travels faster to the area of the brain (amygdala) that deals with emotional responses than to the thinking area of the brain (neo-cortex) which considers the whole picture. If we respond too quickly to the sensory information we get amygdala hijack – an emotional reaction that hasn't been properly processed. Calming strategies give time for the thinking part of the brain to process the situation before we respond. Our thoughts and emotional reactions lead to chemical releases into the bloodstream which bring about physiological changes that accompany angry behaviours. This is related to fight/flight/freeze reactions – blood flow to vital organs increased and muscles prepared for quick response.

Using the Firework Model

- Think of a time when you became very angry.
- Identify the three elements of the firework model:
  1. What triggered the anger?
  2. What were you thinking to power up the anger?
  3. How did you behave?

Activity Linked to Slide 9

Ask participants to recall a time when they became very angry, and then identify the three elements. What triggered the outburst? What were they thinking to power up the anger? How did they behave?

If they are able to recall a very significant event with sufficient clarity, they may even begin to experience some of the original physiological reactions (such as more rapid heartbeat, muscle tension, butterflies in the tummy and so on.)

If any participant is unable to think of a time when they were very angry, they could think instead about a time when someone they know became very angry.

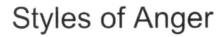

Styles of Anger

- Hostile expression (verbal or physical aggression).
- Passive internalisation (quiet resentment).
- Assertive expression (controlled and considered).

Facilitator Notes for Slide 10

In schools we often treat anger and aggression as somehow synonymous. However, anger does not always involve an aggressive response.

Neither is aggression necessarily an expression of anger. Some children adopt habitually aggressive responses because they achieve a desired outcome (for example, time out and work avoidance, or domination of peers). Learned behaviour is different from a genuine emotional response and is less likely to be helped by anger management training:

- When it is acted out, anger involves verbally and/or physically aggressive behaviour – shouting, swearing, fighting, kicking and so on. In other words, hostile responses.

- If it is not outwardly expressed, it is pushed down inside (internalised). Although it may be easier to manage in school it is not necessarily less harmful. Others may be kept safe, but the person who is angry may risk long-term harm. Anger that bubbles away inside may present as bitterness or depression which, in extreme cases, could lead to conditions such as anorexia or other forms of self-harm.

- Too much aggression or too little expression may both be harmful to our psychological wellbeing. We therefore need to find appropriate ways of managing and expressing angry feelings. Assertive expression would be controlled and thoughtful, showing an awareness of the thoughts and feelings of others while still making clear one's own feelings.

Stages of an Angry Outburst

- **Trigger** – setting events create potential for outburst.
- **Escalation** – fight/flight response kicks in.
- **Crisis** – full-blown anger reaction.
- **Recovery** – internal chemical balance restored.
- **Post-crisis depression** – regret and guilt.

Facilitator Notes for Slide 11

Anger doesn't simply come and go. There is a build-up and aftermath. This has been described by Glynis Breakwell (1997) as the assault cycle.

(These stages will be elaborated on the next slide.)

The assault cycle is what happens when two or more people get into heated conflict with each other. It is a description of the physiological responses that occur. Anger isn't just something that happens in the mind. The whole body is involved and exerts a considerable influence on the situation. The assault cycle is driven by the fight or flight response. This response serves a necessary purpose in our lives.

Trainees could be asked to think of examples in life when 'fight' is the most appropriate response and others when 'flight' is the most appropriate response.

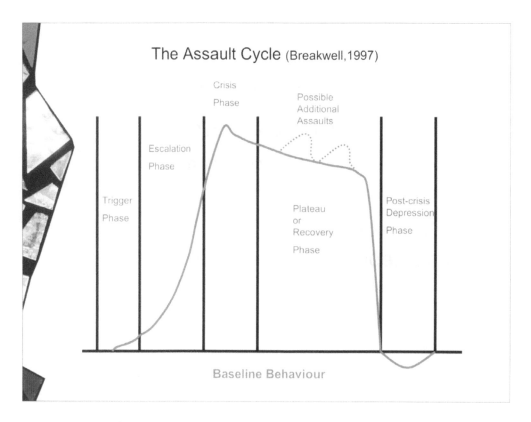

The Assault Cycle (Breakwell,1997)

Crisis Phase

Possible Additional Assaults

Escalation Phase

Trigger Phase

Plateau or Recovery Phase

Post-crisis Depression Phase

Baseline Behaviour

Facilitator Notes for Slide 12

This is a visual representation of the physiological changes that take place when a person becomes very angry. The baseline represents a normal level of arousal. When something occurs to trigger angry feelings, arousal is heightened rapidly. Unless controlled early on in the escalation stage, anger will not be able to be successfully defused.

At crisis stage, the situation has to be managed as safely as possible until the young person calms. The focus is on safety first.

The recovery is slow at first. Although the person may appear calm, chemical levels are still high and it is very easy to trigger further crises (for example, by provocative questioning, punishment, sarcasm). As a child grows older, the time needed to recover becomes longer – especially during adolescence.

If the outburst has been severe the recovery may be followed by a period where the young person feels very low, regretting their actions and perhaps feeling guilty about what they have said or done. At this stage they may beat themselves up mentally or some may even hurt themselves physically.

It is important to note that those witnessing/dealing with the incident are likely to experience a similar pattern of arousal, though less intense.

The next few slides consider strategies that might be appropriate at the different stages of the assault cycle.

Trigger Stage

- Intervene promptly.
- Divert attention if possible.
- Relocate child or other child(ren).
- Give positive directions.
- Allow time for child to take-up directions/suggestions.
- Note triggers and aim to avoid repetition.

Facilitator Notes for Slide 13

Strategies appropriate for the different stages of the assault cycle are listed and explained on the handout, Managing Anger at Different Stages of the Assault Cycle.

This is the stage at which we are most likely to be able to intervene successfully to defuse the situation.

Escalation Stage

- Need to defuse situation quickly.
- Change activity?
- Encourage use of calming strategies:
  - Deep breathing and relaxation.
  - Counting (slowly, in multiples, backwards).
  - Self-talk.
  - Time out.
  - Physical activity.

Facilitator Notes for Slide 14

There is very little time at this stage to get the situation under control. If it isn't defused promptly it will reach a crescendo. Once those chemicals start pumping round the body it becomes much harder to pull back.

Activity Linked to Slide 14

Ask participants to identify strategies that they use or have seen others use successfully.

Crisis Stage

- Safety first!
- Avoid physical restraint unless essential.
- Remain calm:
  - Quiet, slow voice.
  - Simple language.
  - Broken record technique.
- Non-threatening.
- Request help.

Facilitator Notes for Slide 15

At this stage the priority is keeping everyone safe.

Physical restraint should normally be a last resort because it will often make a pupil angrier still.

Be aware of the power of mirroring and be a calm role-model.

Get help from another adult if you need it.

Activity Linked to Slide 15

Seek examples from participants of times they have used any of these or similar strategies.

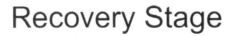

Recovery Stage

- Allow sufficient time.
- Be positive.
- Safe environment.
- Avoid discussion of incident.
- Time out or low demand activity.

Facilitator Notes for Slide 16

The time needed to recover from an angry outburst will be longer as pupils get older. It increases significantly in adolescence.

Even though the young person may look calm on the surface they may still be emotionally volatile. Further outbursts can be easily triggered in the immediate aftermath of the original incident.

Activity Linked to Slide 16

Ask participants if they can provide any examples from their own experience of additional flare-ups during the recovery stage.

Post-crisis Depression Stage

- Reassurance and encouragement.
- Demonstrate personal acceptance despite unacceptable behaviour.
- Avoid adding to guilt.
- Keep lines of communication open.
- Think how to avoid repetition of crisis behaviour (create alternative shared plan).

Activity Linked to Slide 17

Ask participants to think about pupils they know who are prone to angry outbursts. Have they noticed in any of them a tendency to be down on themselves following a serious incident? What kind of behaviours have they noticed?

Discuss this in small groups, then take some feedback from the whole group.

Anger Management Programme

This programme can be used to:

- overcome frequent loss of control
- develop understanding of issues
- present alternative ways of communicating needs/feelings
- recognise the signs of getting angry
- consider range of calming strategies

Facilitator Notes for Slide 18

Where a young person frequently displays angry outbursts that represent genuine loss of control (rather than learned behaviour) they may benefit from a structured programme to develop better management of angry feelings.

An important part of such a programme would be to help them:

- recognise and reflect on their own feelings
- realise that getting angry is not in itself wrong (but can be better managed)
- is a reflection of frustration, worries, fears and so on
- recognise the short-term physical changes that happen in the body during and leading up to an angry outburst
- recognise that anger sometimes gets directed to the wrong people.

Uncontrolled outbursts occur when a child hasn't learned to talk about how they feel and the things they want or need. Learning how to express what really matters to them is an important factor in changing their angry behaviour.

An important part of managing anger is recognising the early warning signs – physical changes in the body. These are the first indication that we need to act to avoid an outburst of anger that might be regretted later.

In the context of all of these other aspects of the programme, possible calming strategies should be explored for different situations.

Evaluate

- Do you have a fuller understanding of anger?

- Do you have some additional ideas about how to manage anger effectively?

- Could you plan a support programme for a child with anger management difficulties?

Activity Linked to Slide 19

Allow a few minutes for participants to reflect together on what they have learned from this session.

Were there any aspects they hadn't thought about before?

Are there any things they want to try to do differently now, either in how they manage their own anger or how they respond to anger in someone else?

What would they want to include in an anger management programme they plan for a pupil in their school? Ask participants to discuss this in their small groups.

Programme Structure

- Normalise anger.
- Base on firework model:
    - Trigger.
    - Fuse (most of the programme focuses at this stage).
    - Explosive body.
- Use firework analogy to analyse incidents.
- Consider impact of behaviour on self and others.
- Reflect on calming strategies.

Facilitator Notes for Slide 20

In an anger management programme there needs to be plenty of time and opportunity to think through the issues:

- There is a risk of children who receive an anger management programme thinking that they are never supposed to get angry, which would be both an impossible as well as an undesirable outcome. Sometimes it's not only appropriate but right to be angry. But we do need to be able to stay safe and keep others safe too.

- The firework model is a helpful analogy upon which to structure a programme. For more detailed suggestions about the programme content, see the chapter 'Understanding and Managing Anger' in *Emotional Wellbeing: An Introductory Handbook* (Shotton & Burton, 2008).

- Once the child understands the stages of this model they can use it to describe specific incidents (for example, 'The trigger was Jack calling me names. The fuse was me thinking about other times he has done this, how much I hate it and that I wanted to hurt him too. I started to get hot and tense. When I exploded I kept punching him really hard until he cried.')

- Some children may not have fully considered the impact their behaviour has on their peers. It may, for example, mean that other children don't push them around, but may also be leaving them isolated or making them unpopular. The section on puppets in the chapter referred to above is relevant here.

- It's important not to impose calming strategies on a child/young person, as they will not all suit everyone. These should be explored to see what they think might work for them or which they would like to try. Some will suit one context but not another, so the young person will need alternatives that fit the different contexts that are challenging for them. There needs to be opportunity to keep practising them and to evaluate their effectiveness, until new responses are well established.

Working with Puppets – Facilitator Notes

The DVD was filmed during a training session delivered by the author to a cohort of trainee ELSAs. Its purpose is to show how puppets may be used differently within any age range to good effect. The DVD has three sections. The first is a general introduction to the rationale behind the use of puppets and discussion of a variety of ways in which they might be used.

Puppets can facilitate the building of relationships with younger children. Where they might be reluctant to talk directly to an adult they may open up more easily when speaking to a puppet, and sometimes also through a puppet.

One of the main advantages of using puppets is the opportunity to externalise sensitive issues so that they might be considered in a non-threatening way by children and young people. By attributing the area of difficulty to a puppet rather than the child, it avoids the natural defensiveness that occurs through direct challenge. The young person is enabled to look at issues with a greater objectivity and begin to consider alternative perspectives that open up the possibility for change.

Puppet role-plays can be used effectively to explore social and friendship skills with primary age pupils. An ELSA and a child could play out, through their respective puppets, scenarios of relevance to the issues being considered. Topics such as sharing, taking turns, asking permission to join a game and managing put-downs are just a few examples.

Animal puppets offer a great opportunity to use metaphor. In anger management work they can be used to represent different relational styles. Sharks and crocodiles, for example, are thick-skinned creatures that are extremely frightening when aggressive. The impact of their behaviour is to alienate others. As humans, we do well to be wary of their unpredictability. There are some people who may have a similar impact upon us as the shark and crocodile. A dragon has similar characteristics, and in mythology is represented as breathing fire. This might be likened to the extreme verbal aggression that some pupils engage in. Yet underneath the thick, protective skin the young people have developed, we do well to remember their vulnerability. By contrast, the spider spins a web to catch its prey. In the school context, we may be able to think of pupils who successfully wind up others but are able themselves to skillfully avoid the attention and recrimination of staff. Snails, tortoises and scallops protect themselves from perceived danger by retreating into their shells, which offer some degree of camouflage in their natural habitats. There are times when maintaining a low profile is safer for us too. There are other creatures that, like us, are essentially social in nature and depend upon each other for their mutual wellbeing. Primates are a good example of this. Monkeys live in colonies where there is a clear social hierarchy that maintains order.

The second section of the DVD features a demonstration of how puppets may be used to provide a greater depth and richness to therapeutic work. Rebecca, a colleague psychologist, is assisted to reflect upon one of her friendship groups. The purpose of this demonstration is to show that age is no barrier to using these resources, and ELSAs are therefore helped to see how work with teenagers may also be enhanced by such resources. Such work is not limited to puppets. Soft toys, miniatures, stones, shells and buttons can all be used in similar ways. They allow the client to look in on their world as if stepping outside of it for a time. Yet in doing so, some surprising thoughts and feelings may be brought out into the open for consideration together.

The final section comprises feedback from the demonstration. Rebecca speaks about the impact the puppets had on her reflections about her friends. The trainee ELSAs are invited to consider the impact the puppets had upon the interaction between facilitator and client. Particularly noticeable is how the use of such resources allows greater space and time to think. The facilitator is able to stay with the thoughts and feelings being expressed by the client without pressure to be thinking of the next question.

This kind of work allows some of our hidden thoughts and feelings to emerge in a powerful way. When children and young people engage with puppets or other representational materials they will inevitably bring something of themselves to the interactions, even if they are not ostensibly the focus of the discussion. This is illustrated in the final moments of the DVD when the author recounts a personal experience of working with a troubled child.

The Firework Model

Trigger:	What were the setting events? Who was there? What happened?
Fuse:	What were you thinking? (What were you saying to yourself? What previous experiences came to mind?) What physical signs did you notice in your body?
Firework:	What did you do? What was the outcome?

Day 3

Managing Anger at Different Stages of the Assault Cycle

Trigger Stage

- Action must be prompt if escalation is to be avoided.

- Distraction can be a particularly effective strategy with younger children and may work with older ones.

- Try to identify trigger and remove child from it if possible. If the presence of others is a provocation, consider moving the child away (or move others away from the child).

- Telling a child what to do is more effective than telling them what not to do, for example, 'Sit at your table…, thanks,' rather than. 'Stop getting out of your seat.'

- Avoid squaring up to the child in a 'do it now, or else…' manner. It's often better to look or move away for a few moments, removing attention long enough to allow the child to make a better choice without losing face.

- Learn from experience. Get to know what the child reacts to and try to avoid those situations. Some children react to being asked to start work. This may indicate expectation or fear of failure. In this case, don't avoid giving work but offer sufficient support to enable them to have a go.

Escalation Stage

- Act quickly because time is running out. If the situation isn't defused promptly it will reach a crescendo. Once those chemicals start pumping round the body it becomes much harder to pull back.

- In some cases a change of activity may be sufficient, especially if the child is frustrated. They may need a short break, for example, to get a drink of water.

- This is the time to use calming strategies:

    - Deep breathing and relaxation techniques require some practice. Some children become more tense when they try this, so practise at a calm time to see whether it's likely to work for them.

    - Simply counting to 10 may be inadequate, especially if done too quickly. If the child has to think about the task they won't be focusing on being angry.

    - Many of us talk to ourselves when stressed, giving ourselves instructions or telling ourselves we can get through this. A catchphrase can be helpful, ('slow down', 'stay cool', 'ignore'.)

    - When highly aroused, time out to calm down may be needed.

Day 3

- Physical exercise is a great de-stressor. That's why some children kick a door or punch a wall, but a cushion or punch bag is safer. If appropriate, a walk or something more energetic may work better.

Crisis Stage

- Once the explosion comes, safety is the paramount issue (both the child's and other people's). Remove dangerous items. You may need to remove the child, or if this can't easily be done, remove the others.

- Physical intervention is usually even more provocative to an angry child, so should be avoided unless absolutely essential for reasons of safety.

- Be aware of your own feelings. As a child's arousal levels rise, so will ours. But injecting further emotion into a volatile situation is highly counter-productive. Generally things will escalate further and the explosion will be worse. We naturally tend to mirror each other, so deliberately slowing and quietening things down tends to have a calming influence. It's harder to continue reacting angrily towards someone who isn't rising to it.

- Strong emotional reactions are controlled from the brain stem, not the cortex (thinking part of brain), so it's no good reasoning at this point. Keep language simple and to a minimum. To keep repeating a simple instruction (like a broken record) can be an effective strategy. In the absence of being able to think what else to do the child will often comply eventually.

- Avoid threats. They are counter-productive because they provide an additional provocation. This isn't the time to give a punishment. The consequences of the behaviour can be discussed once the situation is well past and the child has fully recovered. Be careful not to make fun or let others make fun of the child. This is a very potent threat to their self-esteem and likely to make matters worse.

- If the crisis is severe, it's wise to get help. This is not a sign of weakness. If you have become part of the trigger in some way, another person may be better placed to help calm the child. Or if there are other children around, someone else may take charge of them while you are managing the angry child.

Recovery Stage

- Give the pupil space and time to calm down. There is a danger of assuming, once the initial explosion has ended, that the flare-up is over. Unless adequate time is allowed for the chemical levels in the blood to return to a normal level, further explosions may occur. It doesn't take much – just a look or a comment may do it. Some young people may take an hour to get over an upset, so be patient. Very young children may recover rapidly.

- At this stage it's important to remain positive with the child.

Day 3

- To avoid additional flare-ups the child needs to feel safe. Keep a close eye on what others are doing around the pupil as well as on how the pupil is coping.

- It's still too soon to discuss the consequences of the incident. If you are concerned others will think the child is getting away with bad behaviour, say something along the lines of, 'This is serious but we'll talk about it later.'

- Some children will need time alone at this point to get over the outburst, especially if they are embarrassed by their own behaviour. Sometimes asking them to do a small and undemanding job for you helps them know that you still value them.

Post-crisis Depression Stage

- It's helpful at this point to focus on something positive to help restore their dented self-esteem.

- The child may be anxious that they have burned their bridges with you, so treating them with respect and concern helps to negate that fear.

- They are not yet ready to think through the wider consequences of their behaviour (for example, impact on others). Save this until their equilibrium has been re-established.

- It's important to remain open towards them as their tendency may be to close down at this point.

- Helping the child to come up with a plan to more effectively manage any similar situation in the future (in a way that would feel better for them and others) would provide a positive focus at this time. Work towards a 'win-win' solution. Thinking about 'I messages' (that communicate needs assertively without accusing/blaming the other person) can be useful.

Planning an Anger Management Programme
– Outline of Session Plans

For details of resources listed below see Chapter 10 of *Emotional Wellbeing: An Introductory Handbook* (Shotton and Burton, 2008).

Session 1

Resources:	Game – All About Me (primary). Ungame (secondary).
Session aims:	To develop rapport between ELSA and pupil. To acknowledge that everyone experiences strong feelings and ange normal.
Discussion:	Talk about one time you were angry. Invite pupil to talk about one time they were angry. Anger may be an appropriate response in some situations. Think of examples. Explain that the challenge is to stay safe when angry, and keep others safe too.
Activity:	Brainstorm the range of words that come to mind when we think of anger. Separate them into three groups – physical signs, feelings, behaviours.
Game:	Pre-select the game cards. Begin with the more neutral ones that help you get to know each other. Feed in a few feelings-related cards lower down the pile.
Take-away task:	Remember one good thing that happens during the week and share it with the ELSA next session.

Session 2

Resources:	Game – All About Me (primary). Ungame (secondary). Activity page comprising a list of potential triggers. Diary sheets made into booklet.
Session aims:	To introduce firework model. Explore range of things that trigger angry feelings.
Recap:	Everyone gets angry. Sometimes anger can lead to positive outcomes. The challenge is to manage angry feelings so that everyone stays safe.
Review:	Recall one good thing that happened during the previous week.

Discuss: Firework model, using a picture or 3D model. Talk about the trigger being the things that lead us to feel angry. Those angry feelings usually come because we feel threatened in some way (not necessarily physically; it is often about looking or feeling stupid). Once the angry feelings start, it is as if a fuse is burning. Some people have very short fuses; others may simmer for a while before blowing up. The firework represents us – if we don't stop the fuse burning, we will eventually have some kind of explosion.

Activity: Make a model of a match and firework for pupil to keep. Make a moveable fuse that can be lengthened and shortened.

Activity page: Read through the activity page of potential triggers, identifying which ones are potent for ELSA and pupil.

Game: All About Me or Ungame. Include some cards about feelings and difficult situations this time.

Take-away task: Keep a diary of the week, noting those things that helped each day go well or spoiled the day.

Session 3

Resources: Face It cards.
Visual illusion pictures.
'Managing Anger Successfully' interview sheet (with questions such as 'What makes you angry?', 'How do you manage to stay calm when you feel annoyed?', 'What could I do to avoid losing my temper when I am upset?', 'What things do I do that annoy other people?').
'Thought-Busters' game from A Case for Conflict Resolution.

Session aims: To recognise different emotional states.
To identify the kinds of thoughts that power-up or defuse anger.

Recap: Talk about the three parts of the firework model. Recall some of the main triggers identified in the previous session.

Review: Share the diary of previous week. Look for any link between unhappy days and angry incidents.
Review firework model. Last session's focus was the trigger. This session is about the fuse, particularly how thinking negatively leads to feelings of frustration, stress and anger. If we can manage to look at a situation from a different perspective we can often reduce anger levels.

Day 3

| Game: | Face It cards. These can be used in a variety of ways. Attention should be drawn to facial expression and body language. |

Game: Face It cards. These can be used in a variety of ways. Attention should be drawn to facial expression and body language.

- Pick a card and talk about a time you felt like that.

- Pick a card and mime the emotion for others to guess.

- Play Pelmanism with a selection of the cards. (There are 13 emotions and two cards for each would be needed. For younger groups the number of cards should therefore be reduced.)

Activity: Visual illusions – seeing things differently. Look at each of the pictures and ask the pupil what they see. Then ask if they can see anything else. If not, describe the alternative image that you see. When all the pictures have been viewed in different ways, reflect on what we can learn from this. The pictures don't change, but the way we interpret them can. This isn't only true of visual illusion pictures. The same can be true of events. If, for example, someone bumps into us, we can interpret it as an act of aggression or an accident. How we feel will be different, depending upon which interpretation we choose. Think about alternative interpretations for a range of scenarios, and the feelings that the different thoughts are likely to trigger.

Game: 'Thought-Busters' from A Case for Conflict Resolution.

Take-away task: Ask the pupil to think of someone they know well who usually manages to stay calm when things go wrong, and to interview them before the next session.

Session 4

Resources: Paper and coloured pens/pencils.
Outline drawing of human body.
Anger log sheets (three sections – trigger, fuse, firework).
Game – Overheating (primary).
Anger Solution Game (secondary).

Session aims: To recognise the physical feelings that accompany anger.
To begin to identify some calming strategies.

Recap: Visual illusions show us that people perceive things differently. When we feel angry about something, it is helpful to stop and think about whether there could be a different way of viewing the situation.

Review: Discuss the outcomes of the interview.

Activity: Anger can be accompanied by a variety of physical feelings which can be useful early warning signals to us if we become more attuned to what typically happens within our own body. Ask the pupil to remember a time when they felt very angry. Encourage them to think themselves back to that situation in detail and try to recapture those angry feelings, representing their anger on paper. This may be a drawing of the event or an abstract representation of the emotion. Try to notice any physical feelings (increased heart rate, muscle tension, heat, sweaty palms) and indicate these on the outline drawing of the body. If the pupil has successfully recaptured some of their angry feelings, show them how to take a few slow, deep breaths and relax their muscles to calm themselves. The assault cycle could be explained to older pupils.

Game: Overheating (primary) or Anger Solution Game (secondary).
The purpose of this game is to begin to identify possible calming strategies. As different strategies are identified, ask the pupil whether it is a strategy that might work for them. If so, to what situations would it be suited?

Take-away task: Pupil to keep a log of times when angry feelings occur. Identify the trigger (or setting events), the thoughts that powered-up the anger with any accompanying physical signs, and the actions that resulted (how the firework exploded).

Session 5

Resources: A selection of puppets representing aggressive and non-aggressive creatures.

Session aims: To think about threatening and defensive behaviours and their consequences for self and others (drawing some lessons from the animal kingdom).
To continue thinking about calming strategies.

Recap: When we become angry there are usually some accompanying physical reactions because of chemicals that are released into the blood stream.

Review: Entries in the anger log.

Day 3

Activity: Our behaviour triggers reactions in other people. When we display anger we may provoke anger or fear in others. How we treat others influences their feelings towards us. Taking different puppets in turn, think about whether that creature threatens others, and if so how. When it is threatened, how does it defend itself? (See attached chart.)
Follow-up questions:
- Do you know any people like this creature?

- Which of these creatures are you most like?

- Which would you prefer to be more like?

- What useful defence strategies can we learn from them?

Take-away task: Ask pupil to continue to use the anger log to record times they feel angry, how they deal with those feelings and the outcome.

Session 6

Resources: 'Walking and Talking' game from A Case for Conflict Resolution. Selection of puppets.

Session aim: To practice assertive, non-blaming ways of expressing needs and preferences.

Recap: The way we behave towards others influences the way they behave towards us. Non-aggressive defense strategies are likely to have better social outcomes for us than aggressive ones.

Discussion: Explain 'I messages' as a way of making others aware of behaviours that trigger annoyance and suggesting alternative preferred behaviours. They may be difficult to use in the heat of anger, but are a powerful way of communicating when calm – perhaps in reparative conversations following conflict. The format is 'When people... (name other person's behaviour) it... (name the behavioural response) and I feel... (name own feelings). I would prefer... (suggest alternative behaviour).' For example, 'When people accuse me of doing something I haven't done I react badly. I feel very angry. I prefer them to check out the facts first.'

Activity: Think of some situations that trigger annoyance. Pair up an aggressive puppet with a non-aggressive one. Act out scenarios using 'I messages'.

Game: 'Walking and Talking' from A Case for Conflict Resolution (primary).

Role-play: Create, then role playrole-play, 'I messages' for the following scenarios:

- Name-calling.
- Taking equipment without asking.
- Spoiling a game.
- Someone pushing in front in a queue.
- Being shouted at.
- Being told you can't do something without being told why.

Take-away task: Ask pupil to practice using 'I messages' at home and at school to let people know how they would prefer to be treated. Suggest they keep a note of when they use them and how the other person responds so that this can be discussed next time.

Session 7

Resources: 'Climbing like Mad' game from A Case for Conflict Resolution (primary). Anger Bingo for Teens (secondary).

Session aim: To revise the anger management strategies that have been covered and review progress.

Recap: If we can learn to be politely assertive in our communication with others, explaining what they can do to help us, we may be able to change their behaviour to avoid some of our triggers. 'I messages' are a non-confrontational way of expressing our needs/preferences. Being able to express ourselves verbally reduces the need for confrontational behaviour.

Review: Review the use of 'I messages' since last session and what effect they had.

Game: 'Climbing Like Mad' from A Case for Conflict Resolution (primary). Anger Bingo for Teens (secondary).

Activity: List all the calming strategies that have been discussed during the sessions. Return to original list of triggers (identified in session 2). Ask pupil to choose an appropriate anger management strategy for each trigger. Discuss why a repertoire of strategies is needed. (Walking away doesn't work well when an adult is telling you off, but is very effective when a peer is annoying you. Exercising to let off steam is effective outside but not in class.)

Take-away task: Pupil to practise using the strategies they have chosen.

Day 3

Anger Management – Lessons from the Animal Kingdom

Creature	Reaction to threat (how it keeps itself safe)	How it threatens (what it does when it's angry)	Consequences of its behaviour (outcome of its threatening/ defensive behaviour)
Shark	Has a thick skin, attacks first	Bites (sharp teeth), thrashes tail.	Isolated; induces fear in others.
Bee	Can intimidate or fly away.	Buzzes and circles (intimidates), stings.	Dies once it has stung.
Snail	Retreats into own shell (camouflage).	Doesn't threaten other creatures.	Protects itself from predators; isolated but not feared.
Spider	Runs away fast, rolls into ball to hide, some play 'dead'.	Ambushes prey (some spin webs).	Isolated – other inseccts avoid it.
Scallop	Closes shell tightly (strong muscle).	Doesn't threaten other creatures.	Protects itself from predators; grows pearls inside (hidden treasure).
Mouse	Runs away, can flatten itself to get through cracks.	Only bites if cornered or attacked.	Social – sometimes kept as pet, thought of as cute, not easily caught.
Dragon	Thick scaly skin, attacks first.	Breathes fire, roars, bites, thrashes tail.	Isolated – induces fear in others.
Turtle	Swims away or retreats into own hard shell.	Some only eat seaweed, others small creatures.	Protects itself from predators, not social but not particularly feared.

Communicating through Puppets KS1/2

What to Use

Puppets can be used with individual children, in pairs, in small group work or at the whole class level. You can use:

- your finger with or without a face drawn on it e.g. as a worm
- your hand with or without a face e.g. as a spider or a crab
- finger puppets, bought or homemade
- wooden spoons with wadding and material
- home made felt hand puppets
- glove puppets
- soft toys
- masks

Individual Work

Puppets can be used in 1:1 work to explore areas of difficulty with puppets enables children to think about them in the third person so that they can be discussed less emotively.

Small Group Work

Puppets can be used for work on, for example, friendship skills. Different puppets could help the shark puppet with ways to make more friends; the bee puppet could be helped with ways to manage her anger and preserve her life; the mouse puppet could be given a target to help him to be braver in social situations.

Examples
- A shy puppet who doesn't feel safe joining in: this may help shy children to identify with the puppet and find safe ways to participate.
- A 'younger sibling' puppet who doesn't understand social rules and whom the children can help to socialise.

Puppets could be taken home by a child for the weekend with a sticker chart that the child manages. The sticker chart could incorporate social, behavioural or emotional targets for the puppet to try to meet. This enables the child to try out the teacher/adult role. It can be very empowering and help the child to internalise socially appropriate behaviour.

Whole-class Work

Puppets can be used for Circle Time, PSHE. Children can make their own puppets and create mini dramas around an emotional theme; by using stories built around puppets you can explore issues such as feelings, telling the truth, changes in the family and so on (for example, 'Citizen Cyd' by Eve Wilson; Lucky Duck Publishing Ltd.).

Developing Emotional Literacy

Puppets can be used as an everyday and fun way to develop emotional literacy skills in children both in school and at home. They can be used to help children to understand emotions, to empathise with others, to develop social skills such as listening and turn-taking, to manage angry feelings and to problem-solve difficulties in their social and emotional worlds.

Psychological Benefits

Using puppets can help children to:

- take different perspectives on a problem area

- try out different identities

- internalise socially appropriate roles and behaviour

- assimilate difficult experiences by acting them out in stories or play scripts

- learn how to make good relationships

- learn how to be less impulsive by learning how to think and talk about emotions

- have fun so that they learn better!

Suggestions for Ways to Use Puppets

- Give the puppet a name to suggest their personality.

- The puppet can be an exaggeration for humour and greater impact.

- If you dare you can use a different voice for the puppet so that it appears to take on a life and personality of its own.

- Puppets can take different roles so that children can explore the impact of different ways of behaving for example:

  - A naughty puppet who breaks the rules: the child can be put into the role of helping the puppet to behave better and follow the rules. This helps the child to internalise appropriate behaviour and is empowering because the child is put into the role of the guardian of the rules.

Day 3

- An angry puppet who can only express its angry feelings by being aggressive: exploring this can help children to consider alternative ways of responding, the difference between assertive and aggressive responses, and ways to calm.

Useful contact: www.thepuppetcompany.com
Email: info@thepuppetcompany.com

Adapted from material produced by Sue Sheppard for the Hampshire Educational Psychology Service

Day 3

Communicating through Puppets KS2/3

Developing Emotional Literacy

Puppets can be used as an everyday and fun way to develop emotional literacy skills in children both in school and at home. They can be used to help children to understand emotions, to empathise with others, to develop social skills such as listening and turn-taking, to manage angry feelings and to problem-solve difficulties in their social and emotional worlds.

Psychological Benefits

Using puppets can help children to:
- take different perspectives on a problem area
- try out different identities
- internalise pro-social roles and behaviour
- assimilate difficult experiences by acting them out in symbolic form
- learn how to make good relationships
- learn how to be less impulsive by learning how to think and talk about emotions
- have fun so that they learn better!

What to Use

Puppets can be used with individual children, in pairs, in small group work or at the whol class level. You can use:
- your finger with or without a face drawn on it, for example, as a worm
- your hand with or without a face, for example, as a spider or a crab
- finger puppets, bought or homemade
- wooden spoons with wadding and material
- home made felt hand puppets
- glove puppets
- soft toys
- masks.

Suggestions for Ways to Use Puppets

Puppets can be used with older students to explore feelings, anger management, conflict resolution and social interaction skills. It is helpful if you can use a variety of puppets with different 'characteristics', for example:

Dragon – verbally aggressive.

Bee – bursts of anger.

Clam – very shy.

Shark – physically aggressive.

Snail – shy, unassertive.

Tortoise – quiet, patient.

Mouse – timid, sensitive.

Spider – secretive, manipulative.

The puppets can be used 1:1, with pairs or in small group work. Students could be asked to choose a puppet with which they feel an affinity. The following activities could be used:

1. Using the handout Lessons from the Animal kingdom the following questions could be useful:

- How does your animal defend itself?

For example, the clam, snail and tortoise have a protective shell, which in anger management terms, could be likened to the strategy of keeping a low profile and perhaps erecting an imaginary shield to protect the self from verbal attack.

- What effect does its behaviour have on others?

- What are the consequences of your animal's behaviour?

For example, the bee can only sting once with drastic consequences for itself so it's strategy may be that it is better to fly away than risk death.

- Do you know any people who behave like that?

- Which animal are you most like?

- What is it like for a person with, for example, spider characteristics? The spider spins a web to entrap others. There may be people who behave like this, who manage to stir up others into getting into trouble while avoiding it themselves.

- How could the shark do things differently so that he would be less feared? Sharks tend to be isolated because of their aggression: they make other creatures afraid which mitigates against social contact.

It can be useful to explore with KS3 students how the different animals deal with anger or perceived threats and relate this to different response styles in people including the students themselves.

Day 3

- How could we help the mouse to be less timid?

Mice are not aggressive and live happily in social groups. Their response to threat is to run from danger.

2. Participants could make up role-plays in pairs or write a script for their animal exploring some of the above questions.

3. Issues that could be explored through role-play:
- The difference between assertive and aggressive behaviour.
- The impact of different styles of self-expression on others.
- How to find win-win solutions if there are conflicts.
- Socially acceptable ways to resolve conflicts.
- Strategies for difficult situations.

Useful contact: www.thepuppetcompany.com
Email: info@thepuppetcompany.com

Adapted from material produced by Sue Sheppard for the Hampshire Educational Psychology Service

Day 4

Content and Plan

PowerPoint Presentation – Social Skills Training (slides and notes)

   Supporting Documents:

      1. Set of Sentence Activity Cards (Linked to Slide 9)

      2. Set of Secret Instruction Cards (Linked to Slide 15)

      3. Social Skills Assessment Form (Linked to Slide 28)

PowerPoint Presentation – Introduction to Autism (slides and notes)

   Supporting Documents:

      1. Social Stories – what they are and how they are written

      2. Structure of Social Stories

Day 4

Content and Plan

The development of social skills is the central focus of the fourth day of training. Many difficulties arise in school because pupils have not internalised the cultural norms of interpersonal behaviour. ELSAs will often find themselves explicitly teaching pupils the expectations of social interactions with both adults and peers. The training presentation considers the fundamental importance of interpersonal communication, since social interaction is an innate human motivation. It looks at how new skills are developed and identifies basic skills that should be addressed. Learning is most effective when it is experiential, so attention is given to designing a range of experiential learning activities.

An increasing number of pupils in school are being identified as having social communication difficulties including autism. Because it is important to understand the different thinking style of autistic pupils, an introduction to the nature of autism and the social difficulties associated with it is included on this day.

Social stories were developed as a technique for helping autistic youngsters understand social behaviour and develop social coping skills. In fact they provide a useful approach for all children with underdeveloped social awareness, so guidelines for how to write and use them are provided to round off the penultimate training day.

Essential reading: Chapter 8 of course handbook (Shotton and Burton, 2008).

Suggested timings for the day:

9.15   Review of progress.

9.45   Presentation: Social Skills Training – slides 1-22.

10.45   Tea/coffee.

11.15   Presentation: Social Skills Training – slides 23-29.

12.15   Lunch.

1.00   Presentation: An Introduction to Autism – slides 1-37.

2.30   Writing a social story.

3.00   Plenary.

3.15   End.

Social Skills Training

Social Skills Training

The ELSA Training Manual
Sheila Burton

Facilitator Notes for Slide 1

The following resources are needed for this session:

- The activity page, Social Skills Assessment Form. (Two copies, one for the activity linked to slide 28, one to keep as a master copy.)

- Sets of activity cards (seven in each) linked to Slide 9. Each card has the sentence, 'I didn't say she stole my purse,' with a different word in italics in each to change the meaning.

- Sets of secret instruction cards (six in each) linked to Slide 15:
  - Stare at the speaker.
  - Look at the speaker's ear.
  - Look down at the floor.
  - From time to time look at your watch.
  - Look through the pages of a book.
  - Keep glancing out of the window.

Aims

The aims are to:

- understand the importance of interpersonal communication
- consider how new skills are learned
- explore basic social communication skills
- think about and plan experiential learning opportunities.

Facilitator Notes for Slide 2

This session looks at the importance of interpersonal communication in our everyday lives – both verbal and non-verbal.

We will consider how new skills are learned through demonstration, practice, guidance and feedback.

Specific basic skills that may need to be a focus for ELSA intervention will be discussed.

There will be time in groups to plan some experiential learning opportunities to increase pupils' social awareness.

Why Communicate?

- Why do we need to communicate?

- As a whole group, brainstorm as many reasons as you can why people need to communicate.

- Record on a flipchart.

Activity Linked to Slide 3

This introductory activity will stimulate some initial thinking about the important role of interpersonal communication and will hopefully identify some of the ideas explored on the subsequent slide.

Day 4

Why do we Need to Communicate?

Three basic elements (Schutz, 1988):

1. **Identity** (belonging; involvement and acknowledgement).

2. **Control** (initiating and responding; choosing object and content of interaction).

3. **Acceptance** (making friends and being liked; fitting in).

Facilitator Notes for Slide 4

Schutz (1988) identified three basic elements which encourage our need to communicate:

1. The Need for Identity

Communication within a group is essential to develop a sense of belonging within that group.

It leads to a feeling of involvement and implies recognition for who we are.

2. The Need for Control

Communication enables us to initiate action and respond to others, giving us control within our lives.

We are able to determine who we speak to and what we say.

3. The Need for Acceptance

We have a natural human desire to make friends and be liked.

The need to fit in and be accepted is also important for our survival and wellbeing.

Features of Social Communication

- It is purposeful.
- It can be determined.
- It is adaptable.
- It is co-ordinated.
- It can be improved.

Facilitator Notes for Slide 5

It is purposeful, that is, aimed towards an intended short-term or long-term goal:

- Short-term goals – asking someone in the street for directions; establishing rapport amongst strangers in order to feel more comfortable in a social context.

- Long-term goals – planning and organising a holiday; building a relationship.

It can be determined in that the individual can have a say in when and how to interact, for example, making a telephone call and arranging a visit to a relative, initiating a conversation with someone in close proximity.

It is adaptable, in that different social communication skills are needed in different situations.

They may vary according to who the communication is with (friend, teacher, stranger) and according to the context (casual playground chat, taking part in a school assembly).

It is co-ordinated. Most effective interactions involve body language to complement the verbal message, for example, if giving a compliment, facial expression and posture need to match what is being said in order to sound genuine.

Social communication skills can be developed and improved through practice and positive reinforcement.

They can be broken down into steps and each step practised separately.

Day 4

Purpose of Body Language

- Complements – illustrates what is being said.
- Emphasises – stresses words or phrases.
- Guides – indicates turn-taking in conversation.
- Replaces speech – symbolic representation of words or phrases; ritualised routines that are part of social convention.

Facilitator Notes for Slide 6

This slide highlights some key functions of one aspect of social communication – body language.

We have already mentioned that it can complement the verbal message, for example, hand and arm movements to indicate size or shape.

By moving in rhythm with the spoken word, body movements can emphasise a message visually (for example, nodding and saying 'yes', pointing and saying 'over there', holding forefinger over lips and saying 'sssh').

There are non-verbal signals that guide turn-taking in a conversation, indicating that we have something to say or are handing over for a response.

Posture and gestures can replace the need for words (and in some situations, like scuba diving, that may even be vital). For example:

- 'thumbs up' and 'OK' signs
- smiling and nodding to indicate agreement
- hugging a bereaved friend, communicating sympathy and support without words.

No Words Allowed!

- Get into pairs.
- One of the pair should begin a 'conversation' using only gestures.
- Neither one of the pair may use any words.
- How long are you able to maintain meaningful communication?

Activity Linked to Slide 7

Participants will probably only be able to keep this up for a minute or two before giving up.

Ask for feedback on what kinds of things were able to be communicated.

If they kept to the rules, they probably only managed quite simple, concrete messages. Abstract concepts are heavily dependant upon verbal communication.

Purpose of Spoken Language

- **Communicates** – conveys information, facts, opinions, feelings.
- **Clarifies** – nature of the relationship, status and roles of participants.
- **Guides** – socially accepted norms of conversation – when, what and how of conversation.
- **Fulfils** – meets human need of wanting to be liked by others and to make friends.

Facilitator Notes for Slide 8

We have just considered the purpose of body language, but on its own it is a limited means of communication. This slide highlights key functions of verbal skills, a major element of our social communication.

Words are essential for conveying more specific information. The last activity illustrated the difficulty of communicating specifics without the medium of words.

The style of communication clarifies the relationship. We don't speak in the same way to everyone. Think how differently we would speak if we were a teacher giving directions to a child, a team member requesting help from a manager, or if we were sharing personal information with a trusted friend.

Speech guides interaction in accordance with cultural norms. There are social conventions about what is appropriate to share with whom, and how and when to do it.

- We don't 'drop a bombshell' just as someone is dashing out of the door to an appointment.
- We tend not to share intimate feelings in a formal meeting.
- We usually avoid humour when delivering bad news.

Spoken communication can play an important role in personal fulfilment.

Sensitivity in communication promotes social acceptability and therefore social contact.

Poor communicators may be socially disadvantaged by being ill at ease in the company of unfamiliar people.

Is Meaning More than Words?

- Form groups of seven.
- Each take one card from the pile.
- In turn, read out the sentence, taking care to emphasise the word indicated.
- After each sentence, identify as a group the implied meaning.
- Continue until all seven cards have been discussed.

Activity Linked to Slide 9

For this activity you will need several sets of seven cards, each of which has the sentence, 'I didn't say she stole my purse.' Each card in the set has a different word in italics, to change the emphasis.

This activity shows that meaning is not conveyed by words alone, but by the way in which the words are spoken (or read). It highlights the complexity of language and meanings, and also the potential for misunderstanding in written communication.

Participants could be asked to reflect upon any misunderstandings they have experienced through written messages (notes, e-mails, letters).

Remind participants of the activity in the Active Listening and Communication Skills module when they were asked to estimate the relative importance of language, paralanguage (tone of voice, inflection, pace of speech) and body language – 7%, 38% and 55% respectively.

Day 4

Stages of Skill Learning

- Demonstration – 'This is how you do it. Watch me.'
- Practice – 'Now you have a go.'
- Guidance – 'Watch out for this. Be careful here.'
- Feedback – 'Well done. That was very good.'

Facilitator Notes for Slide 10

In this module we are focussing on social skills and the fact that we can help children learn and develop their skills in this area. Learning a new skill requires a helpful example to emulate and opportunities to practise in a series of steps, with support and encouragement.

It may be helpful to think in terms of a parent developing the skills of their child by encouraging them to help with a household chore, such as laying the table for dinner. The parent shows how it is done. Then the child is given the chance to practise, possibly with verbal prompts. They may need guidance to get the cutlery the right way round. The parent will probably tell them when they have done it right – 'Well done for holding the knives and forks by their handles.'

Stages of Skill Learning

The demonstration should be carried out by a realistic role-model (not necessarily an expert). It sets standards for the skilled performance and shows the child what it is possible to achieve. Learning is enhanced if the child is actively involved.

The skill is broken down into a series of steps that can be practised repeatedly (the components of the skill). A focus on the complete skill is maintained so that the learner remains clear about the end goal (the sum of the components).

Physical, visual and verbal cues are used to prompt a skilled performance. The child is guided through the initial steps to reduce anxiety and fear of failing. Opportunities are provided to practise the complete skill several times unaided to ensure mastery.

Praise and encouragement from others, during practice or after completing the skill, aids recall. Feedback gives a sense of achievement and pride in completing a skill.

NB: Puppets can be a useful method for practising some social skills in a non-threatening way because the focus is shifted from the child to the puppet.

Theoretical Perspectives

- Concept of social interest (Adler & Rodman, 1988 – individual psychology theory).
- Learning through experience
  (Argyle, 1987 – social skills model).
- Recognition hunger
  (Berne, 1975 – transactional analysis).
- Hierarchy of needs
  (Maslow, 1987 – theory of human motivation).

Facilitator Notes for Slide 11

There are many and various definitions of social skills. This slide gives a brief overview of some relevant psychological concepts.

The concept of social interest recognises that the human desire to communicate with others is propelled by an innate social instinct. There is a need to identify collectively with others and value is placed on the concept of 'community'. Think of babies who are born with innate behaviours designed to attract the attention of their carers, such as crying. It has been shown that even tiny babies take turns in 'conversations' of sound and movement.

Human behaviour is predominantly acquired by observing others and following their example. Through modelling, humans can benefit from the experience of others and acquire a new skill more quickly than by trial and error methods.

Humans are essentially driven by a need to be acknowledged by others and this is satisfied by physical recognition (body language such as touch) and psychological recognition (verbal language such as giving a compliment). We have the ability to fully influence how others respond to us in social situations. How we are affects how we are received.

Maslow's hierarchical representation of needs places physiological and safety needs as being more 'potent' (basic and over-riding) than belongingness and esteem needs. Humans have the capacity for self-development and for capitalising on their potential (self-actualisation) if the more basic needs are satisfied.

Day 4

Summary of Key Points

- To belong to and relate to others is a fundamental human need.
- The acquisition of skills is influenced by the example of others.
- Motivation is an important stimulus for initiating action.
- Feedback is an important stimulus for learning to progress and retaining what is learned.

Facilitator Notes for Slide 12

In covering the first two aims of this session we have thought about the innate drive towards social interaction and the influence of other people in shaping our behaviour.

In our work with children and young people we find that social development can be impaired by early life experiences. In extreme cases children may have experienced emotional neglect. In other instances they may have experienced poor social modelling. However for some the difficulties may arise from an underlying social communication disorder.

For whatever reason social skill deficits may have occurred, ELSAs can play a key role in helping children and young people to develop new skills. A warm, accepting relationship can motivate a desire to learn. Encouragement motivates a willingness to keep trying until new skills are mastered.

We will now shift our focus to some specific basic skills that may need to be explicitly taught.

Basic Social Communication Skills

1. Eye-contact.
2. Facial expression.
3. Gestures.
4. Posture.
5. Proximity.
6. Touch.
7. Appearance.
8. Listening.
9. Initiating and maintaining relationships.

Facilitator Notes for Slide 13

Basic social communication skills are the everyday 'bread and butter' behaviours that enable an individual to get along with other people. They provide the essential framework of skills that can be developed over time with regular practice.

Individuals can progress to more complex skills (for example, assertiveness, problem-solving), but unless the basic skills are understood and used these further refinements will be difficult to achieve.

Nine key elements of basic social communication skills have been identified (taken from *The Social Skills Handbook*, (1991) Hutchings, S., Comins, J. & Offiler, J.).

We will look at each of these skills in turn.

Day 4

Eye-contact

- Too much – intrusive and impolite; can be confrontational and aggressive.
- Too little – anxiety and shyness; can indicate insincerity.
- Target – guide pace and co-ordination of conversation; convey interest.

Facilitator Notes for Slide 14

Mutual eye gaze signals interest and a willingness to interact further (lasts approximately one second). If we don't want to talk we look away, for example, in lifts we may look down or find the buttons very interesting!

Appropriate eye contact between two strangers follows this pattern:

Brief eye contact → look away briefly → eye contact again.

This establishes either a positive response (can initiate a conversation) or a negative response (avoiding interaction).

Too Much

Staring makes recipients uncomfortable and is considered rude.

Use of fixed eye contact if angry can be confrontational and aggressive.

Too Little

Excessive blinking or attempting to cover eyes with hands.

Averting gaze – looking down or away.

May be interpreted as anxiety or shyness (reluctance to make contact and interact). Not being able to look someone in the face can also indicate insincerity (having something to hide).

Target

Good eye contact helps to guide the pace and co-ordination of a conversation. It produces useful handover cues to indicate turns in a conversation. Looking away when you have finished talking (often done automatically) signals that it is the other person's turn to speak.

We often focus away from the face when having to think hard about something we are saying, perhaps because reducing social stimulation enhances concentration. Maintaining frequent eye contact signals interest in what the other person is saying.

Learning About Eye-contact

Secret Instruction Cards

- Work in groups of six – one speaker, one listener, four observers. Rotate roles.

- The listener draws a card from the pack and reads the secret instruction without revealing it to others.

- The speaker talks about their subject of choice while the listener follows the instruction on their card.

- The observers try to guess the secret instruction.

- After each card, discuss how it felt.

Activity Linked to Slide 15

Sets of six secret instruction cards are needed for this activity (one set per group):

1. Stare at the speaker.

2. Look at the speaker's ear.

3. Look down at the floor.

4. From time to time look at your watch.

5. Look through the pages of a book.

6. Keep glancing out of the window.

Encourage participants to work as quickly as possible through these cards. If they get stuck on guessing a card, reveal the instruction to the rest of the group and move on to the next.

This is a useful activity for social skills group work (but could be adapted for individual ELSA work by ELSA playing listener and child trying to identify what instruction she is following).

We learn better through experience than by just being told.

Later in this session there will be time for groups to design experiential activities related to other skill areas.

Day 4

Facial expression

Six primary facial expressions:

1. Anger.
2. Fear.
3. Disgust.
4. Happiness.
5. Sadness.
6. Surprise.

Facilitator Notes for Slide 16

Researchers have identified 6 primary facial expressions that are present across cultures:

1. Anger.
2. Fear.
3. Disgust.
4. Happiness.
5, Sadness.
6. Surprise.

There are clearly degrees of each and refinements within these categories.

For example, concern may be a mild form of fear and shock a more intense form of surprise. Pride could be said to be a variation on happiness in that it entails taking pleasure in something.

Facial Expression

- Too much – embarrassing, contrived, distracting.
- Too little – impersonal, aloof, lacking warmth.
- Target – to match emotional tone of conversation/situation, convey understanding.

Too Much

Exaggerated facial expressions may feel overwhelming and this may embarrass a newly made acquaintance or friend. Excessive use of facial expressions may also be perceived as being insincere and contrived, and may detract from what is actually being said.

Too Little

A blank, expressionless face conveying no emotional response is disarming. It may be perceived as impersonal, aloof and lacking in emotional warmth. It fails to provide feedback as to whether the two people are on the same wavelength. People on the autistic spectrum can present as emotionally 'flat' – reading and expressing emotions tends to be an area of difficulty for them.

Target

Appropriate smiling provides positive feedback – 'I like you/I'm interested, please continue.'

Facial expressions should match the emotional tone of the conversation or situation (looking happy in a party atmosphere, looking surprised at the report of strange occurrences, showing sadness or disappointment at bad news).

We may sometimes see children 'smiling' when being told off. What might this be about? Nerves, anxiety?

Sometimes we may 'leak' feelings without being aware. Have you ever been lost in your own thoughts and had someone say to you, 'Cheer up, it might never happen.'?

Day 4

Gestures

- Too much – inappropriate gestures confuse, excessive gesturing distracts.
- Too little – indicates lack of interest or unresponsiveness.
- Target – guides pace of conversation and adds emotional emphasis to it.

Facilitator Notes for Slide 18

Gesture can be intentional (adding emphasis to language) or unintentional ('leaking' emotional state).

Gestures include such movements as head nods, fist-making, rubbing of hands, raised eyebrows.

Too Much

If gestures don't match what is being said they give out mixed, confusing messages.

Excessive gesturing (vigorous head-nodding, flailing arms) may distract from what is being said. Some people's idiosyncratic mannerisms can make it more difficult to concentrate on the content of what they are saying and cause them to become an object of amusement to others.

Gestures are subject to cultural variation and may therefore be misinterpreted across cultures.

Too Little

Lack of appropriate gestures (for example, ritualised routines such as waving goodbye or shaking hands when introduced to a stranger) may be perceived as being uninterested and unresponsive.

Target

Gesture provides interest to what is being said, adding colourful flourishes and illustrations. Appropriate use of gesture helps to guide the pace of conversation and add emotional emphasis to it (for example, stamping foot when angry).

Posture

- Two main positions – tension and relaxation.
- Too much tension - conveys anxiety.
- Too much relaxation – may convey indifference or over-confidence.
- Listless posture – boredom, apathy.
- Target – open and alert.

Facilitator Notes for Slide 19

There are two main postural positions:

1. Tension.

2. Relaxation.

Posture cues (tense or relaxed) convey the nature of relationships within social interaction (for example, pupil going to see the headteacher).

Too much

A very tense posture conveys anxiety and apprehension (for example, sitting on the edge of the chair; stiff, upright posture; tense muscles). It may also make others uncomfortable and nervous.

Inappropriate posture in formal situations may give the wrong impression, for example, an overly relaxed posture in a job interview may be perceived as being indifferent or over-confident.

Too little

A listless posture (drooping shoulders, slouching, head bowed) can be perceived as withdrawn, insular behaviour. It may convey boredom or apathy. It fails to provide encouraging, positive feedback to others.

Target

An open, confident and alert posture indicates a willingness to be approached and to be communicative. Face-to-face interaction is enhanced when face, gaze and body are positioned towards the other person.

Day 4

Proximity

- Personal space – buffer zone in social situations.
- Intimate distance (up to 18in).
- Personal distance (18in-4ft).
- Social distance (4-12ft).
- Public distance (12ft and beyond).

Facilitator Notes for Slide 20

The use of personal space acts as a buffer zone in social situations. It defines a person's 'territory'.

The context of the relationship (and social situation) defines what is a comfortable distance between people. Strangers will tolerate decreased personal space at a football match or on a crowded train.

In non-crowded contexts, sharing intimate personal space (proximity of less than 18in) involves trust and a willingness to be intimate.

Personal distance of 18in-4ft is the usual proximity for everyday social encounters and casual conversations, for example, staffroom.

Social distance of 4-12ft tends to apply to formal encounters at work and more impersonal everyday encounters, for example, in a shop.

Public distance (of 12ft or more) ranges from the distance between a teacher standing to address a class of pupils to the distance between performers and an audience.

Proximity

- Too much – an invasion of privacy, can be perceived as 'pushy'.
- Too little – backing away, or using physical objects as a barrier to closer proximity, conveys a reluctance to interact.
- Target – to match proximity to the nature of the interaction.

Facilitator Notes for Slide 21

Too Much

Disregarding someone's personal space creates discomfort (for example, children who may be described as 'in your face'). It can be perceived as an invasion of privacy and as being 'pushy'. Moving in too close when meeting someone for the first time is likely to cause embarrassment and discomfort.

Too Little

Reluctance for proximity conveys a negative message – a rejection of social contact.

Target

The aim is to match proximity to the development of the relationship and also the nature of the interaction.

Touch

- Neutral body contact – professional relationships; formal greeting.
- Active body contact – more personal and intimate relationships.
- Too much – over-familiar.
- Too little – can seem 'cold'.
- Target – appropriate use of touch in everyday situations.

Facilitator Notes for Slide 22

Neutral body contact occurs within professional relationships (for example, between doctor and patient) and within more formal social relationships (for example, shaking hands when introduced to a new person).

Active body contact occurs within more personal and intimate relationships (parent and child, close friends). It conveys affection or concern, and shared trust.

Too Much

Active body contact in more formal social occasions can cause embarrassment or may be interpreted as being very forward and over-familiar.

Active or neutral use of touch varies between cultures so may be open to misunderstanding or misinterpretation.

Youngsters with learning difficulties are often socially immature and have behaviours that are more acceptable in younger children. Some youngsters need to be taught to refrain from what would be perceived as inappropriate touch.

Too Little

A lack of spontaneous touch can be perceived as being rather cold and unfeeling in certain situations, such as comforting or congratulating a friend.

Target

Appropriate use of touch in everyday situations such as greetings, farewells, congratulating and guiding (for example, offering an elderly person an arm to help them across the road).

We may see older children still using touch that would be more appropriately displayed by a younger pupil. We need to teach them other more appropriate skills.

Planning Learning Experiences

- Divide into five (or more) groups.
- Each group designs an experiential activity for one of these skill areas:
  - facial expression
  - gestures
  - posture
  - proximity
  - touch.

Write on the flipchart and feed back to whole group.

Activity Linked to Slide 23

This activity is likely to need at least 20 minutes to do and at least a further 10 minutes for feedback. Some of these basic skills are easier to design activities for than others, so presenters will need to offer support as needed. (There are some examples in Chapter 8 of *Emotional Wellbeing: An Introductory Handbook*, Shotton and Burton (2008))

Ideas could be typed up and distributed at the next session so that every participant has a record of activity ideas for each skill area.

Appearance

- Dress – may reflect age, status, personality, occupation. May express individuality or mood.
- Inappropriate appearance – undermines belongingness.
- Target – 'looking the part' conveys willingness to fit in and be involved.

Facilitator Notes for Slide 24

Will now look at the last three of our list of nine basic social communication skills.

Style and manner of dress may reflect age, sex, status, personality and occupation. Choice of clothes expresses a person's individuality and may convey mood.

Inappropriate choice of dress can emphasise difference rather than belongingness. It can result in feeling left out or being avoided by others (for example, wearing casual clothes at a formal reception). A neglected personal appearance may be perceived as being uninterested in conveying a positive impression (for a range of reasons).

Appearance has an impact on how children are perceived by other children. Poor hygiene can be particularly problematic and can lead to social isolation. There may be a role for the school nurse in such cases, but ELSAs may also be able to support a child by teaching self-management/hygiene skills. Stories could be used to support this, since sensitive subjects are sometimes more easily addressed by not attributing the issue directly to the child.

Target

Personal appearance has a strong impact when forming initial first impressions. 'Dressing the part'/caring for ones appearance/hygiene conveys a wish to 'fit in' and be involved with others.

Listening

- Hearing – physiological aspects.
- Attending – selective process.
- Understanding – interpretation.
- Remembering – residual message.
- Target – looking at the speaker allows access to non-verbal as well as verbal cues, gives the speaker feedback and reduces outside distractions.

Facilitator Notes for Slide 25

There are several aspects to listening:

- Hearing: the physiological aspect of detecting the sounds.

- Attending: a selective process, attending to relevant information and giving meaning to what is said.

- Understanding: interpreting what is heard with reference to previous knowledge, social context and rules of grammar.

- Remembering: the residual message, that is, the bit that remains and can be recalled.

Difficulties in any of these areas may result in inadequate reception of messages. Being too selective will cause the received message to become distorted. Many children have poor attention skills and are easily distracted.

Target

Looking at the speaker helps in several ways:

- The listener picks up non-verbal cues that enrich the spoken message.

- The speaker receives feedback signals from the listener (and can check understanding).

- The listener is less likely to be distracted by other sights and sounds.

Day 4

Initiating Relationships

- Coming together – exploration, acceptance, compatibility.
- Too eager – may be alarming.
- Too reticent – missed opportunities.
- Target – identifying shared interests or common experience.

Facilitator Notes for Slide 26

Finally, we will think briefly about initiating and maintaining relationships. We will focus in more detail on friendships during our final training day.

Building a relationship involves stages of 'coming together':

- Exploration – establishing common ground.

- Acceptance – developing trust and understanding.

- Compatibility – increased rapport, closeness and sharing.

We tend to develop friendships with those we meet often and can easily identify with.

There needs to be a mutual desire to develop a relationship – rushing in too eagerly may be overwhelming and alarming for others.

Holding back too much may prevent potential relationships from developing.

A starting point may often be a shared interest or common experience. Initially small talk helps to break the ice and establish a comfortable atmosphere in which more significant conversations may develop.

Maintaining Relationships

- Mutual involvement.
- Self-disclosure.
- Empathy.
- Positive regard.

Maintaining relationships often relies on:

- Mutual involvement. Remaining physically accessible (for example, living nearby, being at the same school, being involved in common activities) helps to keep the relationship going.

- Self-disclosure. This involves sharing factual information about oneself, opinions and feelings. It helps to build trust, but needs to be at an appropriate pace.

- Empathy. The ability to put yourself in the other person's shoes and understand their perspective without being judgmental and moralistic builds rapport. Having similar backgrounds, attitudes, values and interests can help in creating empathy between people. If a child's own needs are not being met it is difficult for them to develop this skill.

- Positive regard. Having a positive opinion of another person despite differences between you. Showing positive regard would include a:
  - cheerful attitude
  - helpful manner
  - friendly tone of voice
  - approachable and attentive posture
  - providing positive feedback (smiling, agreeing, making appropriate comments).

Showing positive regard gives the other person the feeling that they are worth getting to know and that they matter. We tend to seek out people who give us positive 'vibes'.

We have now covered our list of nine social skills. Children within our schools can lack skills in one or a number of these areas. An ELSA's task is to identify weaknesses and plan support accordingly.

Day 4

Prioritising

- Using the Social Skills Assessment Form, rate a child you know well on each skill listed.

- Prioritise the areas to work on.

- From the activities devised in groups, choose one or more that might be useful in working with this pupil.

Activity Linked to Slide 28

There is a variety of assessment tools available which can help you plan the focus for your support to enhance a pupil's social competence.

The Social Skills Assessment Form (provided) is one such tool.

Use the Social Skills Assessment Form to consider a child you know well. By highlighting relative strengths and weaknesses you will be helped to prioritise areas of focus for intervention. The last group activity should have given you some ideas for experiential learning opportunities to promote greater skill in these areas.

References

- Hutchings, S., Comins, J. & Offiler, J. (1991) *The Social Skills Handbook*. Bicester: Winslow Press.
- Schutz, W. (1988) 'The Interpersonal World' in Adler, R. B. & Rodman, G. (eds) *Understanding Human Communication* (3rd ed) London: Holt, Reinhart & Winston.
- Adler, R. B. & Rodman, G. (1988) *as above*
- Argyle, M. (1987) 'Some New Developments in Social Skills Training', in Mayor, B. M. & Pugh, A. K. (eds) *Language, Communication and Education.* London: Croom Helm.
- Berne, E. (1975) *Transactional Analysis in Psychotherapy*. London: Souvenir Press.
- Maslow, A. H. (1987) *Motivation and Personality* (3rd ed). New York: Harper & Rowe.

Facilitator Notes for Slide 29

These references are provided for those who may wish to explore further any of the theories mentioned earlier.

Day 4

Set of Sentence Activity Cards

✂

'**I** didn't say she stole my purse.'

'I **didn't** say she stole my purse.'

'I didn't **say** she stole my purse.'

'I didn't say **she** stole my purse.'

'I didn't say she **stole** my purse.'

'I didn't say she stole **my** purse.'

'I didn't say she stole my **purse**.'

Set of Secret Instruction Cards

Stare at the speaker.	Look at the speaker's ear.
Look down at the floor.	From time to time look at your watch.
Look through the pages of a book.	Keep glancing out of the window.

Social Skills Assessment Form

Name: ....

Date: ....

Completed by: ....

Teacher: ....

Pupil: ....

Parent/Carer: ....

Tick the appropriate number by each social skill.

Skill	Very Poor 1	2	3	4	Very Good 5
Listening without interrupting					
Paying attention when spoken to					
Making eye contact					
Following directions					
Sharing					
Taking turns					
Asking for help					
Ignoring teasing and provocation					
Following rules of play					
Expressing own emotions					
Expressing own opinions					
Handling success					
Handling failure					
Speaking in a pleasant tone of voice					
Using appropriate body language					

Day 4

Slide 1-37

Introduction to Autism

An Introduction to Autism

ELSA Training Manual

Sheila Burton

Facilitator Notes for Slide 1

For this session, you will need to prepare a selection of social stories suitable across the age range represented by trainees.

Day 4

Aims

The aims are to:

- understand the nature of autism
- explore some key theories
- raise awareness of their difficulties
- explain the use of social stories and how to write them.

Facilitator Notes for Slide 2

A module on autism is included in the training because ELSAs are likely to support children on the autistic spectrum. In order to support their social communication needs it is important to understand the different thinking style of autistic children.

Some of the key theories about this difference will be introduced and consideration given to the challenges autistic children face in coping with school.

Social stories have proved to be a very useful technique for helping autistic children to understand and develop social behaviours which enable them to participate in aspects of everyday life they find challenging.

'History' of Autism

- First described by Leo Kanner, 1943.
- Summarised the case histories of 11 children.
- Listed a number of unusual characteristics common to each.
- Hans Asperger, 1944, recognised a pattern of abnormal behaviour in a group of adolescents.
- Understanding has been refined over time, recognising variations in degree of autism.
- More prevalent in boys than girls.

Facilitator Notes for Slide 3

Disorder first described by Kanner in 1943. He summarised the case histories of 11 children and realised they had a number of unusual characteristics in common.

At around the same time, Hans Asperger recognised a pattern of abnormal behaviour in a group of adolescents which he called autistic psychopathy. The term Asperger Syndrome is now used to describe those with higher functioning autism who are more linguistically able.

Over subsequent decades researchers have come to realise that there are large differences in the extent to which people are affected by autism.

There are many more cases reported in boys than in girls.

Day 4

Cause

- Remains unknown.
- Wolff (1988) suggested:

  '…for autism to develop, brain damage has to occur in the setting of a genetic predisposition. The causation of autism, which is likely to be heterogeneous, arises when a number of possibly quite common factors coincide, and it is the coincidence that is rare and makes autism uncommon.'

Facilitator Notes for Slide 4

Despite extensive research we still do not know what causes autism.

Wolff suggests that there might be a variety of contributory factors which come together to create what we know as autism.

Diagnosis

- No identified gene (unlike many syndromes).
- Relies on behavioural observation.
- Diagnosis via Health Service.
- Usually a long waiting list for assessment.
- Terminology – autistic spectrum disorder/continuum (ASD/ASC)… recognising degrees of autism.

Facilitator Notes for Slide 5

No gene identified, unlike many syndromes.

Diagnosis relies on behavioural observation.

Often long waiting lists for medical diagnosis.

The term 'autistic spectrum disorder' has often been used, and now 'autistic spectrum continuum', recognising that there is a continuum of difficulties.

Day 4

Nature of Autism

- Developmental (emerges over time).
- Organic (biologically based).
- Lifelong.
- Areas of difficulty:
  - social relationships
  - communication
  - language
  - cognition
  - learning.

Facilitator Notes for Slide 6

The condition becomes apparent over time (not usually recognised before the toddler years and often later).

There are believed to be differences in the brain.

The condition doesn't go away.

It shows itself in:

- social difficulties (relating to others)

- communication difficulties (understanding and expression of thoughts, feelings, emotional state... non-verbal and verbal)

- language problems (receptive and expressive)

- cognitive problems (do not think in same way as non-autistic people)

- learning problems (the above factors will impact learning, and some autistic people have significant learning difficulties).

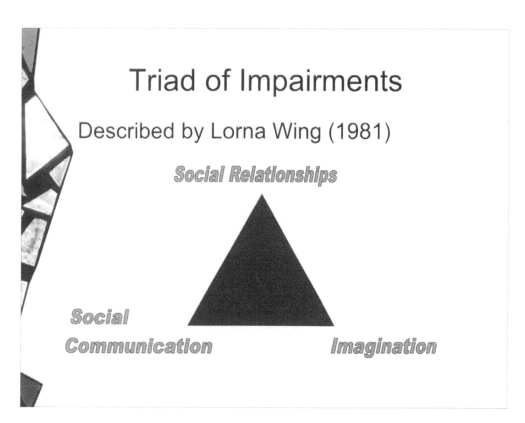

Triad of Impairments

Described by Lorna Wing (1981)

Social Relationships

Social Communication

Imagination

Facilitator Notes for Slide 7

Lorna Wing described autism as a triad of impairments of social interaction:

- Difficulties in relating to other people.
- Difficulties in communicating with other people (including both expression and understanding).
- Difficulties in the area of imagination.

Day 4

What Does it Look Like?

- Have you known any children with autism?
- In which ways have they been different from others?
- Discuss your experiences in a small group.

Activity Linked to Slide 8

This is an opportunity for participants to discuss together (in small groups) their experience of autistic children and young people. There is no need to take feedback as key features will be explored in subsequent slides.

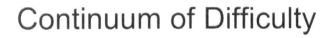

Continuum of Difficulty

- Wing expounded notion of a continuum.
- Lower functioning children frequently show abnormal responses to sensory stimuli with repetitive movements, such as flapping or hypersensitivity to noise.
- Higher functioning children sometimes possess an area of exceptional skill.
- Asperger's Syndrome – more able/verbal.

Facilitator Notes for Slide 9

It was Lorna Wing who first expounded the idea of autism as a continuum of difficulty.

The least able children tend to manifest abnormal responses to a greater degree.

Sometimes there can be an area of exceptional ability, for example, artistic, musical, unusual memory skills in a certain area.

Those with Asperger's Syndrome tend to be of higher ability and more verbally skilled. The difference between Asperger's Syndrome and high functioning autism relates to early language skills.

Day 4

Impairment of Social Relationships

- Difficulty with social empathy
- Continuum of difficulty:

1. aloof and indifferent
2. approaches for physical needs only
3. passive acceptance of approaches by others
4. approaches on own terms

Facilitator Notes for Slide 10

The most severely affected appear to treat people as objects.

Others actively avoid physical contact and don't seek comfort when distressed, but may approach others in order to get a physical need met, for example, have something done for them.

Others passively accept approaches but tend not to actively initiate them.

The least severely affected make contact on their own terms, to satisfy their own needs and interests, and are less likely to engage in contact for the sake of others. Relationships are not reciprocal (based on mutual interest) which leads to difficulties in sustaining friendships.

Impairment of Social Communication

- Lack appreciation of social uses of communication (talk *at* not *with*).
- Lack understanding of purpose (sharing information with others).
- Poor understanding and use of non-verbal communication.
- Understanding and use of words tends to be concrete and literal.

Facilitator Notes for Slide 11

Autistic children fail to take account of the listener's responses when talking. They may, for example, talk at length about something of personal interest without picking up any cues that the listener's interest has been exhausted.

There is a failure to see language as a tool for passing on and receiving information of mutual interest. They use it merely to express their own needs.

Their poor appreciation of meaning behind non-verbal cues such as facial expression leads to social disadvantage.

Figures of speech are interpreted literally, for example, 'pull your socks up', 'get a grip', 'till the cows come home' and so on. Our language is rife with such non-literal idioms.

Day 4

Impairment of Social Communication

Severity ranges from:

no communication at all

spontaneous use of speech and gesture,
repetitive and one-sided.

Facilitator Notes for Slide 12

In most severe cases, there is a failure to even respond to their own name, and no desire to talk.

In milder cases, spontaneous use of speech and gesture but this can tend to be repetitive and one-sided (meeting own needs).

Any absence of gestures only applies to those related to mental states (for example, consolation, embarrassment) and not to behavioural gestures, for example, come here, be quiet, go away (Attwood et al, 1988).

Autistic children don't use pointing to share attention, but do use it to get a desired object (Baron-Cohen, 1989).

Impairment of Imagination

- Lack of imaginative play (use of an object to represent something else).
- Tendency to select details and not understand meaning of the whole scene.
- Routines copied somewhat mechanically – lack of genuine 'shared' play.
- Lack of creativity – thinking rather literal and inflexible, making fiction and poetry inaccessible.

Facilitator Notes for Slide 13

There is a lack of pretend or creative play. While other children could imagine a large cardboard box to be a boat, for example, to the autistic child it remains a box.

They could be fascinated by spinning the wheels on toy cars but have no interest in the cars themselves.

May appear to be playing imaginatively but the play tends to be a repetitive, mechanical routine.

The autistic child has difficulty letting others intervene in play. They are unable to share. Insists on controlling what others do in play.

Their thought patterns are very literal. There is no appreciation of metaphor. Factual books are preferred to fiction. Fiction tends to use more colourful and symbolic language, playing perhaps with words. Poetry is likely to be very confusing.

Day 4

Impairment of Imagination

Clare Sainsbury described impairment of imagination as:

'...problems with flexible thinking, leading to problems coping with change and a need for rigid routines, and difficulty imagining what other people may be thinking.'

(Martian in the Playground, 2000)

Facilitator Notes for Slide 14

Clare Sainsbury (a Cambridge graduate) wrote about how it feels to go through the education system when you are autistic. She drew on her own experiences as well as those of other high functioning autistic adults.

She refuted the notion that autistic people have no imagination... they may indeed be able to enter their own make-believe world, but their imagination is different from non-autistic people.

In '*Children Can Learn with their Shoes Off*' (Maines, B. 2002), Rita Jordan wrote, 'They can play at being Batman but they cannot play Batman and Robin.'

Other Autistic Features

(Common but not essential)

- Language difficulties – receptive and expressive delay, echolalia, flat tone, poor control of volume.
- Visual inspection – examining from a strange angle (peripheral vision).
- Abnormal eye-contact – looking past people, avoiding eye-contact, staring fixedly.

Facilitator notes for Slide 15

Explain that these will not all be present in autistic children. More severely affected youngsters are likely to show more of these features.

Invite participants to question anything they don't understand rather than talking in detail through each point.

Day 4

Other Autistic Features

- Stereotypical movements
  – flapping, rocking.
- Abnormal responses to sensory
  experiences – touch, sound, light, pain.
- Inappropriate emotional reactions – lack
  of reaction or over-reaction.
- Obsessional interests.
- Special skills ('islets of ability').

Facilitator Notes for Slide 16

Allow time for participants to read and ask any questions.

How Does this Match Your Experience?

- Which of these features have you seen?
- How have you responded to these behaviours?
- Discuss in small groups.

Activity Linked to Slide 17

Participants can discuss in small groups the features (listed on previous slides) that they have personally encountered.

Theory of Mind

- A current psychological theory of autism (Frith, 1989).
- 'Theory of Mind' – appreciating other people's intentions, needs, desires, beliefs.
- Hypothesised that autistic people lack 'theory of mind'.
- Baron-Cohen used the Sally/Anne Test to investigate Theory of Mind.

Facilitator Notes for Slide 18

There has been considerable argument about the possible common link underlying autistic disorders.

In recent years there has been particular interest in Uta Frith's 'theory of mind' explanation.

Autistic children may have a particular problem understanding that people have mental states which can be different from the state of the real world, and different from the autistic person's own mental state. We could refer to these as 'belief systems'.

Baron-Cohen used the Sally/Anne test to check children's ability to see things from another person's point of view.

The Sally/Anne Test

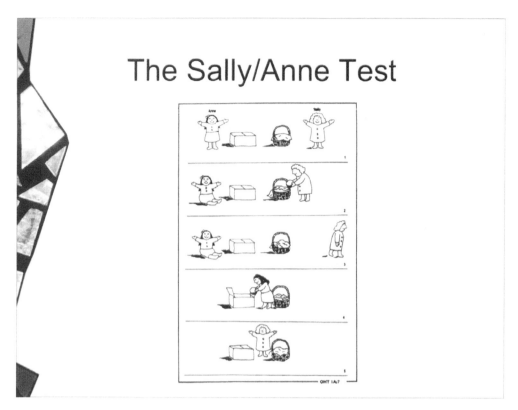

Facilitator Notes for Slide 19

Sally puts the ball in the basket then goes away.

Anne transfers the ball to the box.

Sally returns. Where will she look for the ball?

The Sally/Anne Test

- Baron-Cohen compared responses of three groups of children using this test:
  1. Autism with mental age (MA) over four years.
  2. Down Syndrome with MA over four years.
  3. Normally developing four year olds.
- The autistic group thought Sally would look for the ball in the box.
- The others thought she would look in the basket.

Facilitator Notes for Slide 20

He compared the responses of three groups of children matched for mental ability.

Only the children with autism said Sally would look in the box. The others said she would look in the basket, where she left it.

This theory could explain not only some of the deficits associated with autism, but also why some skills are unaffected.

Any skill requiring only primary representations should be unimpaired, thus allowing for islets of ability and good rote memory.

You In Their Shoes...

- Think about how it might be for you if you could only ever see things from your own perspective.

- What sort of difficulties might you encounter as a pupil in school?

- Discuss in pairs or small groups.

Activity Linked to Slide 21

Ask participants to take a few minutes to think and talk about how they might experience life in school if they had no appreciation of any reality beyond their own understanding. This is an opportunity to experience a little bit of empathy for an autistic child in the school community.

An Autistic Adult's Experience

'Autism isn't something a person has, or a "shell" that a person is trapped inside. It is pervasive, it colours every experience, every sensation, perception, thought, emotion, and encounter, every aspect of existence. It is not possible to separate the autism from the person – and if it were possible, the person you'd have left would not be the same person you started with. This is important, so take a moment to consider it: autism is a way of being.'

(Jim Sinclair, 1993)

Facilitator Notes for Slide 22

This quote, by an autistic adult, emphasises the difference in experience, thinking and emotion between autistic and non-autistic people. It is an appeal to be understood as qualitatively different, rather than someone to be changed.

Difficulties for Autistic Pupils

- Changes in routine (creating anxiety).
- Sharing others' interests.
- Seeming to be 'in a world of their own' (focusing on own interests).
- No intuitive grasp of social hierarchy.
- Analytical rather than holistic thinkers ('weak central coherence' theory) – hard to determine what is/is not relevant.

Facilitator Notes for Slide 23

Because of their rigid thinking, changes in routine are very stressful for autistic children.

Their difficulty in seeing things from other people's point of view makes it hard for them to share other people's interests.

They can be single-minded in their own pursuits and reluctant to be re-focused on to something else.

They tend not to differentiate between people according to status, so may talk in the same terms to a headteacher as they would to peers.

'Weak central coherence theory' has been postulated to explain why they are able to focus on details without appreciating the whole picture. This makes it difficult to determine relative importance and may cause them to be unduly concerned by what others see as irrelevant details. Failure of others to appreciate the importance of these details may lead them to become stressed.

Day 4

Difficulties for Autistic Pupils

- Predominantly visual learning style (often).
- Auditory processing difficulties.
- Literal interpretation of language.
- Intrusive sensory distractions.
- Distractions from within (thoughts).
- Switching attention on demand.
- Accessing memories of events (harder than accessing memories of facts).

Facilitator Notes for Slide 24

Because of their language/communication difficulties, they often tend to be more visual rather than auditory in their learning style. This means it is easier for them to process information that is delivered visually than information that is told to them. Too much language can be overwhelming.

Our language is full of idioms and metaphors which are a source of considerable confusion to the autistic child.

Sensory distractions may be overwhelmingly powerful for them and therefore much more difficult to tune out.

Similarly, their own internal thoughts may be highly distracting, which is why they are sometimes thought to be in a world of their own.

This makes it very difficult for them to switch attention on demand. If they have become very interested in what they are doing, it is harder for them to stop than it is for other children. This difficulty can be misconstrued as being stubborn or awkward. They may need a system of warnings to assist transition from one activity to another.

Their memory for facts is better than their memory for things that have happened. They may therefore be thought to have extremely good memory in some respects and yet be surprisingly blank about other things.

Difficulties for Autistic Pupils

- Organisational ability.
- Motor co-ordination.
- Close physical proximity to others.
- Making and sustaining friendships.
- Becoming victims of bullying (because of their difference).

Facilitator Notes for Slide 25

The ability of autistic children to organise themselves tends to be poor.

Sometimes they may present as rather clumsy.

They feel uncomfortable if they are too close to others. The stress this creates may result in physical aggression.

Because their whole way of thinking is so different and so focused on their own interests, it is much harder for them to make and keep friendships.

They can often be victimised by others because their speech and their behaviour seem odd to others.

Need for Friendship

- Do autistic children want friends?
- Do they need friends?

Discuss in small groups, drawing upon your own encounters with autistic children.

Activity Linked to Slide 26

Ask participants to think about whether the social difficulties autistic children experience indicate a lack of desire for friendship.

Do they have a need for friends?

Rather than right or wrong answers, this is an invitation to think beyond the surface characteristics.

Supporting Autistic Pupils

Pupils are better in formal setting with limited free movement around room. Be aware of potential stressors. Possible adaptations are:

- personal work base in quiet corner of room, possibly partially screened
- removal of distracting materials from nearby
- predictable routine to school day.

Facilitator Notes for Slide 27

The next three slides list some of the helpful adaptations that may support autistic children in the classroom. There is no need to talk through these strategies which are listed for reference.

The remit of ELSAs is more likely to be supporting youngsters to develop specific coping skills in social contexts.

Supporting Autistic Pupils

- visual prompts (for example, individualised timetable with removable activity cards).
- careful preparation for changes in routine (for example, supply teacher, school visits).
- equipment labelled and kept in same place.
- modification of stressful activities.
- increased individual support.

Facilitator Notes for Slide 28

More general classroom support strategies. Allow time for participants to read the slide.

Supporting Autistic Pupils

- Allow for preferred learning style (for example, from visual materials rather than auditory input).
- Use special interests as motivators.
- Teach feelings vocabulary, social and friendship skills in a structured way.
- Avoid rhetorical questions, metaphors and sarcasm.
- Consider peer support approaches.

Facilitator Notes for Slide 29

The third bullet point is one that is likely to require ELSA support.

Learning to recognise and name feelings, in themselves and others, may be a key area of work.

Social and friendship skills will need to be explicitly taught, and social stories will be one useful approach for this work.

Social Stories

Social stories are used for targeting:

- particular situations where the pupil experiences difficulties (for example, playground, assembly)
- new situations which might 'throw' the pupil (for example, changing classes or schools).

Facilitator Notes for Slide 30

Social stories are a helpful way to develop children's understanding of expectations in situations that they find troublesome.

They are also a very effective way of preparing pupils for change and are often used to good effect around transition to a new class or school.

Their usefulness is certainly not restricted to autistic children. They can be helpful for any child who finds change unsettling.

Read and Discuss

- Read the examples of social stories provided.

- Discuss with the person next to you why you think they needed to be written.

- What do you notice about their style?

Activity Linked to Slide 31

Provide a selection of social stories for different age groups.

One useful source of stories is *Writing and Developing Social Stories* by Caroline Smith (2003).

Ask participants to identify the kinds of behaviours that might have required these stories to be written.

Ask them to identify what is distinctive about their style.

Day 4

Writing a Social Story

- A social story describes very specifically **what** happens and **why**, and usually tells the child the desirable way to behave.

- It is written in consultation with pupil/parents/adults and after careful observation of target situation.

- The vocabulary and presentation should be appropriate to child's age and ability.

Facilitator Notes for Slide 32

For a brief summary of the elements of a social story see page 93-94 of *Emotional Wellbeing: An Introductory Handbook* (Shotton and Burton 2008).

Writing a Social Story

- Usually written in the first person and present tense. Can be personalised by appropriate inclusion of pupil's interests.
- Should be attractive and interesting.
- Not a simple list of what to do – include sentences describing **where** a situation occurs, **who** is involved, **what** they are doing and **why**. Also describe and explain reactions and feelings of others.

Facilitator Notes for Slide 33

These stories have a very personal style.

Bearing in mind what has been said about general preference for a visual learning style, good use of illustrations is very helpful. Sometimes it may be appropriate to get the child to produce some illustrations themselves.

Avoid making the story sound like a list of instructions (see next slide).

Day 4

Writing a Social Story

- Basic social stories use three types of sentence:
  1. Descriptive.
  2. Perspective.
  3. Directive.
- Ratio – there should be 3-5 descriptive and/or perspective sentences to every directive sentence.

Facilitator Notes for Slide 34

The story should contain three types of sentence:

1. Descriptive – what happens, where the situation occurs, who is involved, what they are doing and why.

2. Perspective – describes the reactions and responses of others in the target situation, sometimes the reasons for their responses, and may describe the feelings of others.

3. Directive – describes desired responses to social situations. They tell the child in positive terms what he or she should try to do or say in the target situation.

Writing a Social Story

- Words such as '**usually**', '**sometimes**' and '**probably**' are often used to help the child avoid over-literal interpretation and cope with exceptions.
- Stories are only as long as they need to be (keep to the point).
- Generally end with a positive affirmation.

Facilitator Notes for Slide 35

As children with autism often interpret language literally, it is important to avoid statements that are inflexible. It is preferable to use terms such as, 'I will try to…' rather than 'I can…' or 'I will…' both of which are definite statements.

To avoid the child being overwhelmed or confused by language, keep the stories simple. It is better to write separate stories for different issues than try to put too much into one.

A positive affirmation (for example, I am a good girl, I am a hard worker, I am a helpful boy) helps the child feel good about themselves while learning new behaviours.

Day 4

Using the Story

- The pupil reads the story (or listens on audiotape) before the target situation arises, for example, daily before playtime/assembly.

- Daily access to the story should continue as long as the pupil wants or needs.

- It can be re-visited as the need arises.

Facilitator Notes for Slide 36

Use the story as often as necessary until the new behaviour becomes part of the child's repertoire and hang on to it in case the child needs a future reminder.

Create Your Own!

- In a small group, identify a child with a difficulty that might be addressed through a social story.

- Create an outline plan, taking account of the child's age.

- Consider how you would make it visually interesting.

Activity Linked to Slide 37

Allow 20-30 minutes for this activity. Having a go with support will give participants greater confidence to create bespoke social stories for children they support in their ELSA role.

Day 4

Social Stories

Writing Social Stories for Young People with Social Communication/Autistic Spectrum Difficulties

What is a Social Story?

- A social story is a short story written in a specific style and format.
- A story that describes what happens in a specific social situation.
- It describes what is obvious to most of us, but not obvious to those with impaired social understanding.
- The social story describes what people do, why they do it and what are common responses.

What is the Purpose of a Social Story?

Social stories are often used to reduce anxiety and develop appropriate behaviour.

'The goal is to teach social understanding over rote compliance, to describe more than direct.' (Carol Gray, Morning News)

Social stories have been used to meet individual needs in the following situations:

- To provide positive feedback to a young person – to help him to recognise his/her own appropriate skills and behaviour (affirming stories).
- To help a young person prepare for a new experience.
- To help a young person accustom himself to a situation, task or experience and to respond appropriately (developing tolerance and new skills).
- To help prevent extreme reactions which stem from a lack of social understanding and difficulty with imagination.

Features of Social Stories

- They are written for (and with) an individual about a situation, which he/she finds difficult.
- They are based on a careful assessment of the situation.
- The writing is suited to match the understanding and vocabulary levels of the young person.
- They usually include drawings, pictures or photographs.
- They are written in the first person, and present or future tense.
- One aspect or step is often presented per page.

How do Social Stories help?

- They provide accurate information about real and relevant situations.
- Information is presented visually.
- They do not rely on interpersonal contact.
- They provide a prompt about how to respond.
- They provide reassurance.
- They provide positive feedback.

Structure of Social Stories

Types of sentences used in social stories:

Descriptive sentences: These describe what happens, where, who involved, what they are doing and why. They use 'usually' and 'sometimes', not 'always'.

Example:

'There is a lift at the Swan Centre.'

'The lift takes people up and down.'

'Sometimes there are lots of people in the lift.'

Perspective sentences: These describe the reactions/responses of others in the target situation, sometimes the reasons for their responses and the feelings of others.

Example:

'People are usually quiet in the lift.'

'People like it when it is quiet in the lift.'

Directive sentences: These describe the desired responses to the social situation. They are written in positive terms, and will use 'try' to do or say, not 'I can...' or 'I will...'. Absolutes and inflexible statements are avoided.

Example:

'I will try to stand still.'

'I will try to be quiet in the lift.'

Day 4

The ratio is usually at least five descriptive and/or perspective sentences to one directive sentence.

There is a more advanced social stories formula, which depends on the young person's level of functioning and understanding. This can include co-operative sentences and control sentences.

Co-operative sentences: These will answer the question of how others will help the young person to succeed.

Example:

'My mum will help me to be quiet.' 'My mum will give me my slinky.'

Control sentences: These answer the question of how the young person can help himself to succeed.

Example:

'To help me be quiet, I will try to bounce my slinky up and down.'

Sharing the Completed Social Story

Introduce it at a distraction-free time.

It is usual to sit slightly behind and to one side of the young person. This varies according to his/her needs.

When introduced, the social story is usually read at least once a day, and always just before the situation it is addressing.

This may reduce as the social story is internalised. Let the young person be involved in decision-making.

With thanks and reference to:
Gray, C., Arnold, S. & Pauken, S. A. (revised edn) (2001) The New Social Story Book. Arlington, TX: Future Horizons Incorporated.
Carol Rowe (1999) 'Do social stories benefit children with autism in mainstream primary schools?' British Journal of Special Education, Vol. 26, No. 1, pp12-14.
Caroline Smith (2003) Writing and Developing Social Stories. Milton Keynes: Speechmark Publishing.

Jo Birbeck, Hampshire Educational Psychology Service.

Day 4

Day 5

Content and Plan

PowerPoint Presentation – Friendship Skills and Therapeutic Stories (slides and notes)

Supporting Documents:

1. Circle of Friends: Circles – (Linked to Slide 6)

2. Circle of Friends: Process – (step by step guide to process)

3. Circle Meeting – (step by step guide to initial meeting of circle of friends)

Day 5

Day 5

Content and Plan

The final day of training develops the theme of social skills by focusing specifically on friendship needs. There are two parts to the morning session. The first explains a popular intervention known as Circle of Friends. It is helpful for ELSAs to understand the full process even if their involvement is limited to being facilitators of the friendship circle. Some, however, might feel confident to lead the first part with the peer group as well, especially if they have an opportunity to see it modeled by an educational psychologist or experienced teacher first. Circle of Friends was developed in Canada by Pearpoint et al (1992) and introduced widely in Great Britain by Newton, Taylor and Wilson (1996).

Some principles for leading group work are considered, since ELSA intervention on friendship skills may often involve setting up a friendship group. Guidelines are given for planning such work, and time is allowed for some collaborative session planning with colleagues who work with pupils of a similar age.

The afternoon introduces the very useful technique of therapeutic stories for helping pupils consider sensitive issues that they may find difficult to discuss in a direct way.

For further information on how to use therapeutic stories see Chapter 7 of Shotton and Burton (2008). The clinical psychologist, Doris Brett, published two books of stories that she developed for her own daughter, to help her develop coping strategies for the challenge of various childhood anxieties and life events. In the first she included detailed explanation of the process of creating therapeutic stories, (Brett 1986.) Time is allowed for participants to work together on planning a therapeutic story that explores a sensitive issue for a pupil they know.

By the end of this day ELSAs should have been made aware of which supervision group they are assigned to and the date, time and venue for the first meeting. They should be given a copy of the policy document on supervision (a sample policy is included with the supporting documents in Chapter 4). It is vital that they understand the essential nature of clinical supervision for the work they are undertaking, and that this is the way they will receive continuing professional development. Supervision is not an optional extra but a fundamental expectation within this project.

Essential reading: Chapters 6 and 7 of course handbook (Shotton and Burton, 2008).

Suggested timings for the day:

9.15	Review of progress.
9.45	Presentation: Friendship Skills and Therapeutic Stories – slides 1-14.
10.45	Tea/coffee.
11.15	Presentation: Friendship Skills and Therapeutic Stories – slides 15-19.
12.15	Lunch.
1.00	Presentation: Friendship Skills and Therapeutic Stories – slides 20-24.
2.30	Feedback of story ideas created by participants.
2.45	Explanation of supervision expectations and arrangements.
3.00	Plenary.
3.15	End.

Slides 1-24

Friendship Skills and Therapeutic Stories

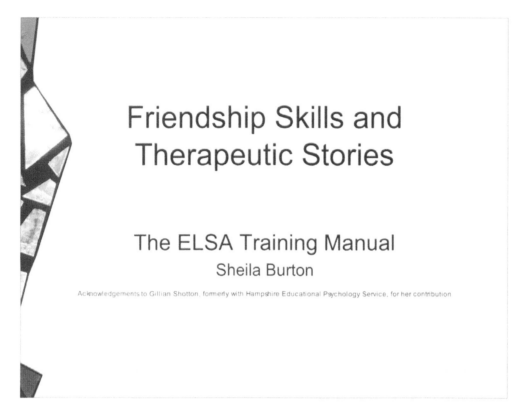

Facilitator Notes for Slide 1

For this session, you will need to prepare the following activity pages:

- Circle of Friends Circles.
- Circle of Friends Process.
- Circle Meeting.

You will also need a selection of therapeutic stories suited to different ages.

Day 5

Aims

The aims are to:

- explain Circle of Friends –
  an intervention to support an individual pupil

- consider friendship skills group work –
  setting up groups, planning session content

- introduce therapeutic stories –
  how to use them and how to write them.

Facilitator Notes for Slide 2

Explain the different components of this final day of training.

The first part of the morning will be spent introducing Circle of Friends – a methodology for setting up a support group for a pupil who is rather isolated. The process will be explained step by step. An alternative approach (a variation on the original) will also be suggested for use where an individual does not wish peer attention to be explicitly drawn to their needs.

The rest of the day will be more activity based.

Developing friendship skills is an area where an ELSA is likely to incorporate some group activities, so attention will be drawn to important factors for consideration when setting up group work. Time will be allowed before lunch for some collaborative session planning with colleagues who work with pupils of a similar age.

The focus of the afternoon will be on therapeutic stories. The principles behind their use will be explained and time allowed for ELSAs to begin planning a story to address an area of need in a pupil they know. This too can be done in pairs or as a small group.

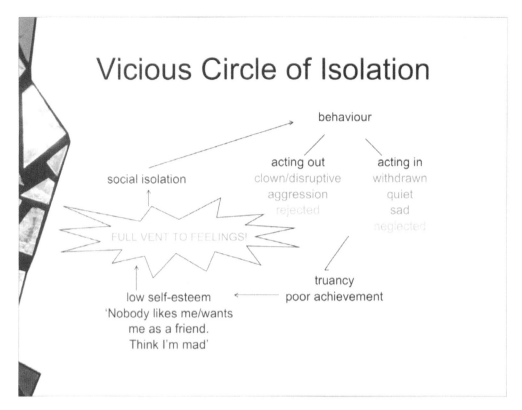

Vicious Circle of Isolation

behaviour

acting out
clown/disruptive
aggression
rejected

acting in
withdrawn
quiet
sad
neglected

social isolation

FULL VENT TO FEELINGS!

truancy
poor achievement

low self-esteem
'Nobody likes me/wants
me as a friend.
Think I'm mad'

Facilitator Notes for Slide 3

Talk through how this happens in practice.

Socially isolated children may handle their isolation by what we call 'acting out' or 'acting in' behaviour.

Those who 'act out' may try to gain attention by playing the clown or they may be verbally/ physically aggressive towards peers and adults. Either way, they are very noticeable, but their behaviour doesn't make them popular. They tend to be rejected and this is likely to continue over a significant period of time.

Those who 'act in' are much less likely to be noticed. They are easily overlooked – neglected.

Isolated children – show higher levels of truancy, under achievement and mental health problems.

Their self-esteem is low, and their response to that low self-esteem (anger/aggression or turning in on themselves) reinforces their isolation from their peers.

The Circle of Friends approach is a very effective way of breaking this vicious circle. It provides the child with a peer group that includes them in school life, reverses their sense of loneliness, raises their self-esteem and reduces the need for the self-defeating behaviours.

Day 5

Circle of Friends: Background

- Technique to create friendship network for isolated pupil.
- Approach is neither 'within-child' or behavioural.
- A systemic response to need.
- Recognises and makes use of pupil culture.
- Low demand on resources.

Facilitator Notes for Slide 4

This approach was introduced to the UK in the mid 1990s by educational psychologists in the Nottingham area (Newton, Taylor & Wilson). The approach originated in Canada as a way of including children with special needs within their peer group in mainstream schools. It is based on the social psychology of acceptance.

The approach isn't predicated on the child's need to change in order to fit in, and isn't based on a system of rewards and punishments designed to alter the child's behaviour – even though changes may be part of the outcome. It is a response to a child's need involving those who are around him/her each day.

Unlike many interventions, it is peer support rather than an adult trying to bring about change. Pupils can often be more motivated to respond to peer support than to intervention from members of staff. Adult input is relatively small.

The Circle of Friends (original approach) will be discussed in detail. Attention will be drawn to an alternative Circle of Friends approach where the 'target' pupil is not identified (Gillian Shotton 1998).

Circle of Friends has been used successfully with pupils of all ages from infant through to secondary school. The process would be the same but led in an age-appropriate way.

Circle of Friends: the Process

- **Prior to starting**:
  - parental permission
  - pupil permission and understanding.

- **Whole class without target pupil**:
  - introduce lesson and ground rules
  - strengths and difficulties of pupil.

Facilitator Notes for Slide 5

It is important to explain the approach to parents/carers and ensure that they are in agreement before following this process.

Pupils also need to understand what is proposed and be happy for their needs to be talked about with their class.

The class work is done without the focus pupil present to avoid embarrassment and enable peers to talk freely. This part needs to be approached very sensitively, seeking agreement from the class to observe confidentiality about what is said (avoiding playground gossip).

The class will take its lead from the facilitator of the session, so positive attitudes and non-blaming language need to be modelled.

Strengths may be presented as interests and abilities they have noticed as well as characteristics they appreciate about the pupil (what things are going well for this pupil?).

Difficulties may be framed as those things that are not going so well for the pupil or things that the class might like to be different for the pupil. This has a very different feel to, 'What is wrong with John?'!

The Circles Exercise

Using the Circles activity page, add the names of significant people in your life:

1. Circle 1 – the people closest to you.
2. Circle 2 – the people you feel close to, but not as close as in circle 1.
3. Circle 3 – the people you know a little bit (from groups you are part of, for example, work colleagues).
4. Circle 4 – the people paid to be in your life.

Activity Linked to Slide 6

Ask participants to fill in the blank Circle of Friends Circles activity page for themselves. This would be done in the same way with children in the target pupil's class or alternatively could be done as a whole-class exercise on a flipchart.

1. Circle 1 usually contains immediate family members.

2. Circle 2 usually contains close friends and extended family members.

3. Circle 3 tends to include people we see regularly (classmates, those we know from clubs and activities) but who are not close friends.

4. Circle 4 includes teachers, LSAs, family doctor, dentist and other such professionals.

Feelings and Behaviours

- How would it feel if circles 2 & 3 were empty?
- Brainstorm a list of feelings.
- Brainstorm a list of possible behaviours.
- Compare with the list of pupil's difficulties and look for similarities in behaviour.
- Could some of the pupil's behaviour be because she feels she doesn't have friends?

Facilitator Notes for Slide 7

This part of the process promotes empathy by encouraging peers to think how they would feel if they felt somewhat alone in a social group. (If the task were done as a whole class on the whiteboard, the contents of circles 2 & 3 could be physically rubbed out. On paper they could be crossed out.)

It's useful to write up the feelings that are suggested.

The next step is to consider the types of behaviour pupils think they might show if they felt isolated.

Attention is then drawn to similarities between the list of their possible behaviours and some of the difficulties that have been identified for the pupil.

The class is encouraged to think about those similarities and why they might be. The skill as a facilitator is to help classmates to make the connection for themselves rather than informing them that the pupil's behaviour is because he/she lacks friends. The idea is treated as a hypothesis rather than a fact.

Responding with Help

- Brainstorm ways that everyone could help.
- What things *wouldn't* be helpful?
- Seek volunteers for Circle of Friends.
- Thank the class and remind pupils that everyone can help to make a difference.

Facilitator Notes for Slide 8

Once the idea has been raised, the class can be encouraged to think of ways in which everyone might be able to make a difference. Check out suggestions to ensure general agreement over what is likely to be welcome support and what the pupil might find intrusive or insensitive.

Explain that a number of volunteers are being sought to be part of a closer support group – people who would genuinely like to get to know the focus pupil better. Generally half a dozen would be enough, and a mixed gender group is helpful. Names could be taken and a final choice made later, or the choice could be made at the time. Some of the most successful groups have included pupils who might not initially seem the obvious choice. Bear in mind the mix of the volunteers and their likely influence on the focus pupil. Be sure to include peers the pupil is likely to want to be with.

There may be some disappointment that not everyone who wants to can be part of the small group, so it's important to reiterate the ways in which everyone in the class can support the pupil.

ELSAs may not necessarily be the ones doing the initial whole-class session (and certainly they would be likely to benefit from seeing it modelled before attempting such a session themselves) but they will be ideally placed to run the follow-up group meetings.

First Circle of Friends Meeting

- Welcome the pupil to group.
- Ground rules and confidentiality.
- Aims of the group:
  to help the pupil make friends, cope well in school, keep out of trouble.
- Each volunteer tells the pupil why they want to be his/her friend.
- Each volunteer says something positive about the pupil.

Facilitator Notes for Slide 9

Bringing the focus pupil and the support group together is often an exciting moment for all, but there may also be some apprehension on the part of the focus pupil and the supporters.

The ground rules need to be established so that everyone can feel more comfortable about how to manage being part of the group.

The aims of coming together should also be made explicit, and are likely to vary from pupil to pupil, depending upon their needs. Some may have behavioural difficulties in school. Some may have learning difficulties. Others will simply be isolated. This can be a very helpful intervention for pupils who are new to the school and finding it hard to become established in the peer group.

It is often useful to give a brief summary of the whole-class session to the focus pupil at the start of the first circle meeting. It's affirming to hear the positives and, if sensitively framed, he or she can often acknowledge the difficulties that have been raised. Warn the group members beforehand that you will ask them to say why they want to be part of the group. This is very encouraging for the focus pupil.

Naming positive attributes reassures the pupil that he/she is valued for who they are.

First Meeting: Actions

- Brainstorm what volunteers want to help the pupil with.
- Brainstorm ideas/strategies for coming week.
- Choose a name for the group.
- Provide drinks and biscuits.
- Set a date for the next meeting.

Facilitator Notes for Slide 10

This is an opportunity to explore what everyone can do to help. It can be useful to make a note of agreements to follow-up at the next meeting whether these things happened and how helpful the focus pupil found them.

It's best for the group not to adopt the pupil's name (John's group) but for members to democratically choose an unrelated name. This avoids the impression that the focus pupil is 'in charge'.

Refreshments at the end of group meetings are nurturing and show that participation is valued. They also provide an opportunity to practise appropriate social skills (requesting, offering, thanking, turn-taking, sharing and so on).

Wherever possible, meetings should be weekly at the same time and in the same place. This provides security by establishing a clear routine and communicates that the group is valued.

Circle of Friends: Weekly Meetings

- What has gone well during the previous week?
- What did not go well?
- What could have been done differently?
- What to focus on next week?

Facilitator Notes for Slide 11

Each meeting provides opportunity for a review of the previous week and a chance to do any problem-solving/new planning that is needed.

Potential Issues

- Over-watchfulness of circle – pupil feeling 'crowded'.
- Others resentful of not having their own circle.
- Members feeling responsible for pupil and over-anxious.
- Over-dependency of pupil on circle.
- Pupil using circle to manipulate others.

Facilitator Notes for Slide 12

These are some potential difficulties that can arise from time to time. It is the role of the facilitating adult to watch out for these and manage them sensitively.

Discuss briefly some possible ways of managing such difficulties should they arise.

Activity Linked to Slide 12

Ask participants to suggest some possible ways of addressing such difficulties.

Potential Issues (cont)

- Pupils making disclosures that are hard for others to hear.
- Pupils wanting to leave the group but feeling guilty/anxious.
- Target pupil feeling rejected if someone wants to leave the group.

Facilitator Notes for Slide 13

If difficult issues are introduced to the circle, the group should be reminded of the confidentiality ground rule, and a suggestion made that the pupil talks on their own with the facilitator at a separate time.

Sometimes it becomes apparent that a volunteer is not committed to the group or no longer wants to participate. In such cases, the volunteer should be asked if they would like to now be swapped out and be thanked for their contribution. Another volunteer could be added in their place – perhaps one of the original volunteers who wasn't chosen initially.

This will need to be handled sensitively with the target pupil, helping them to understand that it doesn't mean the group member doesn't like them or won't sometimes want to do things with them.

Day 5

Adaptation to Circle of Friends

- Target pupil not singled out to class but aware that she is the target
- Friendship facilitated in a more subtle way.
- Focus is on need of everyone in class to establish and maintain friendships.

Facilitator Notes for Slide 14

This adapted approach is described by Gillian Shotton (*Educational Psychology in Practice*, Vol. 14, No 1, April 1998).

In this case, circle meetings would not focus explicitly on the target pupil but would encourage mutual support and encouragement in a less direct way.

This approach would be very appropriate within the context of whole-class work on friendship.

Setting up a Friendship Group

- Selecting pupils.
- Choosing the right group (5-7 members).
- Parental permission.
- Time and place.
- Juice and biscuits.
- Planning the content of the sessions.

Facilitator Notes for Slide 15

It is important to think carefully about the make-up of the group. If this group is being established as a strategy to develop the skills of one particular pupil, try to include children that the target pupil would like to be friends with. But a group may be established because there are two or three children who have difficulty establishing or sustaining friendships. It is helpful nevertheless to include some good role-models.

Once you have identified potential group members, ask yourself whether you can imagine this combination of children working together well. Be careful about including children who show particular antipathy towards each other. Participation should be voluntary.

It may be wise to seek parental permission, particularly if the group is going to take place in lesson time. However, be careful how you do this so that parents don't get the message that there's something really wrong with their child! (If the school doesn't get any response from parents, members of the school staff still have the right to work for the benefit of their child within school if the school management team deems this appropriate.)

When embarking on group work, it is important to have an appropriate venue – preferably the same place and time each week as otherwise you will waste valuable time rounding up the group members!

Sharing refreshments at the end of a session is an important part of the group process. It gives members the message that they are valued. Giving food and drinks is a nurturing activity. It's also a good opportunity to reinforce social skills.

Careful planning needs to go into the content of group sessions:

- Warm-up.
- Revision of previous work.
- A clear aim for the session.
- Varied activities that facilitate learning (these should be interesting and fun).
- Something to go away and practise.

The Skills of Friendship

Discuss in small groups:

- What qualities do *you* appreciate in *your* friends?
- What skills are needed in friendship?
- What do the children need to learn?

Activity Linked to Slide 16

Following discussion, record their ideas on a flipchart.

These represent the kind of skills that you might focus on in a group.

Examples of Qualities

Listen to you, interested, kind, understanding, encouraging, make the effort to keep in touch, give cards/gifts on special occasions, offer help when needed.

Necessary Skills

These include noticing and caring about others (empathy), openness (sharing own thoughts and feelings), loyalty/reliability (not blowing hot and cold), helpfulness.

What the Children Need to Learn

How to be flexible and share friends, how to listen to one another, how to find out about others' interests, how to give eye contact, take turns and so on.

Planning a session

- Decide on group name.

- Outline aims of the group, for example, to help one another become better friends.

- Identify objective for each session, for example, to practise taking turns.

- Agree ground rules, for example, when someone speaks we look and listen, we are kind to each other, what we talk about stays within the group

Facilitator Notes for Slide 17

Choose a name for the group that is non-stigmatising. You might involve the group in choosing the group name. The name gives them their own group identity.

Be clear about the aims for the group.

Each session should have a clear focus, with activities that support the objective.

Ground rules agreed at the outset allow you to address any inappropriate behaviour with reference to those rules. Persistent disregard for the rules would then be taken as an indication that the pupil does not want to be part of the group and could then be addressed accordingly.

Planning a Session

- Warm-up activity.

- Acts of kindness log (optional extra).

- Focus activity (games and puppets are very useful).

- Task for the week.

- Group photo.

- Certificates at the end of the final session.

Facilitator Notes for Slide 18

Here are some ideas for inclusion in a session:

Warm up activity – use something fun, for example, copy me 'clap, clap, click, click' , wink murder, sentence completion, for example, 'If I were a boat I'd be a... because...', memory game, for example, 'I went shopping and I bought...'

Acts of kindness log is a little booklet contained in the friendship skills book for them to copy and use. It makes a good 'homework' activity (although you might not want to call it homework!).

Pupils really enjoy playing games because it makes the session very different from lessons and some of them never sit down and play games at other times. Games give the opportunity to practise some important social skills.

Puppets can be used at all ages – even KS3 pupils have been known to enjoy them! Obviously how you use them will vary with age.

Worksheet activities can be used to reinforce concepts discussed, but should be used sparingly. Keep any writing to a minimum because it can be a turn-off for many pupils.

It's helpful to set a task for the week. It helps new skills to be generalised to life outside the group.

A nice touch would be to take a group photo so that everyone can have a copy at the end of the group. Or it could be incorporated into the certificate. Children value certificates, so make them good quality (preferably laminated).

Start Planning!

- Get into small groups with others who work with children of a similar age.
- Have a go at planning some possible sessions for a friendship skills group.
- Think back to the essential skills that you listed earlier.
- Look at the resources available to help you with ideas for sessions.

Activity Linked to Slide 19

For the rest of the morning, work with a few other people and begin to plan a friendship skills group. It's up to you whether you choose to plan one or two sessions in detail or whether you devise an outline plan for a whole course, for example, about six sessions.

Remember to include a variety of activities within sessions. Think carefully about the progression from one session to the next.

Look at resources on display to give you some ideas.

Therapeutic Stories

- Help a pupil to discover possible solutions to their difficulties and worries.
- Allow them to look at difficulties more objectively.
- Use a central character who faces difficult yet similar situations, for example, *Walter Learns to Enjoy School*, written for a child showing difficult behaviour in school.

Facilitator Notes for Slide 20

Explain what therapeutic stories are. See Chapter 7 of *Emotional Wellbeing: An Introductory Handbook* (Shotton and Burton 2008). A further useful resource is Shotton's *Therapeutic Stories – Stories for Troubled and Troubling Children* (2004, Eddie McNamara's Positive Behaviour Management series.) Read the story of *Walter Learns to Enjoy School* to see how a story was used to reduce a child's challenging behaviour in response to anxiety about school work.

Therapeutic Stories

Help pupils to:

- see things from a different point of view
- recognise and acknowledge different behaviours
- understand *why* they behave in a particular way
- appreciate how their behaviour affects others
- learn better coping strategies to bring about positive change.

Facilitator Notes for Slide 21

Select and read stories written for different ages to exemplify these points.

Tips for Making Up Stories

- What is the difficulty that has created the need for the story?
- What ideas do you want to communicate to the child? What solutions do you want to suggest?
- Start the story with a hero or heroine who has similar difficulties/fears to the pupil.
- Use the plot to suggest a potential solution for the hero/heroine.

Facilitator Notes for Slide 22

Before embarking on writing a story, clarify its purpose in your own mind.

Plan what you want to include. Don't try to address too many issues in one story or it will lose its focus. It would be better to write a series of stories around one character to address different issues. Consider in advance what potential solutions it might be helpful to suggest.

Choose a character that will have appeal and relevance for the pupil. For younger pupils the character need not necessarily be a person. Animals, vehicles, computers and machines have been personified in stories.

The plot should explore the difficulties in a way that allows the pupil to identify at some level (even subconsciously) with the character.

The climax of the story should provide a plausible solution for the central character that may lead the pupil to consider alternative behaviours in their own situation. If you are unsure about whether you have come up with a good solution, the end may be left open (no outcome stated).

Story-making Tips (cont)

- If you are unsure why the child is worried in a particular situation, use questions in the story to gain insight.
- What if the child tries the solution in the story and it doesn't work for them?
- Make sure vocabulary and length are age-appropriate.
- Add illustrations.

Facilitator Notes for Slide 23

Stories can be written in an interactive format. (Why do you think Billy was scared to walk home?) When a pupil offers suggestions on behalf of the story character, they will almost certainly draw on their own thoughts, feelings and experiences.

If one solution doesn't work, you could adapt the story to offer an alternative strategy. You could perhaps suggest the original strategy didn't work too well for the story character either and explore together some alternative ideas for the character to try. View these difficulties as discussion opportunities and see which ideas the pupil most warms to. Therapeutic story-writing can be a collaborative exercise between ELSA and pupil.

You don't need to be a skilled writer. Write with the pupil in mind and you are likely to find you express ideas in ways that are accessible and interesting to them.

Pictures bring a story to life. You don't have to be artistic, just a creative thinker! Clip art is a rich source of illustrations. Many pictures can be found via the Internet. Photos and magazine illustrations are another possibility. The pupil might like to be involved in the search – or even draw their own.

Day 5

Have a Go!

In pairs...

- Think about a difficulty experienced by a pupil one of you knows fairly well.
- Talk about an idea for a story that might help the pupil think or act differently.
- Write a brief story plan.
- Have a go at writing the first part of the story.
- When questions arise, problem-solve with the trainers!

Activity Linked to Slide 24

Allow at least half an hour, but preferably longer, for ELSAs to have a go at writing a therapeutic story together. As a plenary, invite one or two to share their stories or story plans.

Circles of Friends: Circles

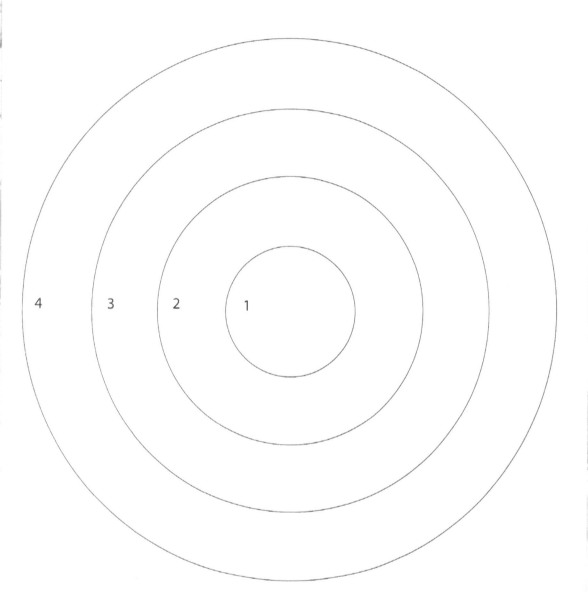

Circles of Friends: Process

Step 1: Whole Class (Named Pupil Not Present)

One approach:

1. Introduce self and ground rules.
   - When one person is speaking, we all listen.
   - We all act sensibly during session; no silliness.

2. Need to talk about (named pupil).
   - Very special session, unusual to talk behind people's backs.
   - We need your help!

3. Need for confidentiality – what does this mean? (Conversation with class)

4. What do you think is happening to (named pupil)?

What do you think about his/her behaviour? Tell us your opinion.
(a) Flipchart results.

Give some words to describe (named pupil) and their behaviour.
(b) Flipchart results.

5. We need your help.
   We need you to work as a team with your teachers.

6. Focus on pupils' own lives.

Circles Exercise

Circle 1: smallest circle:
   - People who love you most.
   - Why did you put those people in circle one?
   - What do you do with people in circle one?
   - How do you feel about these people?
   - How do those people feel about you?

Circle 2:
   - People who are not quite as close as circle one.

Circle 3:
   - Groups of people in your life – scouts/clubs/church groups/teams and so on.

Circles of Friends: Process (cont)

Circle 4:

- People paid to be in your life – teachers, doctors, hairdressers.

7. Show circle – with only a few friends in.

8. How would you feel if your life looked like this? (Flipchart 'feelings'.)

9. How would you act? (Flipchart behaviours.)

10. Look for links between lists 4(b) and 9 above.

11. What can we do to get (named pupil) back on track?

List ideas

....

....

....

....

We need a special group to work with (named pupil) to help her back on track and to help her gain friends and keep them.

Volunteers?

Six/seven, boys and girls.

Circle Meeting

Step 2: Small Group of Volunteers (Named Pupil Present)

1. Introductions/ground rules.
   - When one person is speaking, we listen to them.
   - We all act sensibly during session.

2. The aims are to:
   - work with (named pupil) to help her make friends, to behave well/keep out of trouble
   - support each other in helping (named pupil).

3. Why are you here? Each group member is asked to tell (named pupil) why they want to be in the group. Expand/repeat comments along lines of, 'So you are here to help (named pupil)...'

4. Positives and negatives about (named pupil).

Think of some good things about (named pupil).

Some words to describe (named pupil).

5. What makes you have a miserable day at school? What makes you unhappy/angry? How do you behave when you feel like that?

6. How would you feel if no-one liked you and you had no friends at school? How wou you behave? Compare lists.

7. What can we do to get (named pupil) back on track?

   - What would make her feel more happy?
   - What would keep her out of trouble?
   - What cheers you up on a miserable day?
   - What out-of-school things could you do together?

8. Name for group (not the name of the pupil), for example, 'The Listening Group'/ 'SWAT group'

9. Next meeting – next week.

Day 5

Supplementary Training

Providing Continuing Professional Development for ELSAs.

Loss and Bereavement (slides and notes)

Supplementary Training

Providing Continuing Professional Development for ELSAs

Five days of initial training has been considered optimal but it is recognised that there will be need for further training input from time to time. Occasionally this might be delivered within a group supervision session. Alternatively periodic training development days or ELSA conferences may be arranged to contribute to professional development.

Because ELSAs often find themselves needing to support pupils to cope with issues of loss and bereavement, a training presentation on this topic is included. While bereavement is the main focus, this presentation acknowledges that there are many kinds of loss other than death that may occur during childhood, and that any of these can have a significant impact upon emotional development. The grieving process is considered, with two different models being presented. Practical ideas for responding to bereavement are explored.

Another area that warrants supplementary training is attachment theory and the impact of insecure attachment on children's development. Some of the most behaviourally challenging pupils in school have grown up without the support of a caring adult who is sensitively attuned to their emotional needs. We know that consistent behaviour management alone will not be sufficient of itself to address their needs. The quality relationships that ELSAs are able to offer can do much to help such young people develop a degree of trust in adults. This is an area that probably warrants a whole day of additional training to do justice to the subject.

Another topic worthy of consideration for all ELSAs are the principles and techniques of solution focused brief therapy. Similarly some general principles regarding the link between thoughts, feelings and behaviour that are recognised within cognitive behaviour therapy are worth exploring. It would also be appropriate to have an awareness raising session about the needs of young carers.

Those working with secondary pupils may need some support to understand eating disorders and other self-harming behaviours. It is not expected that ELSAs would have principal responsibility for working with those young people who have complex needs in this area, but some awareness of the topic would increase their confidence in supporting young people who may be beginning to experiment with such behaviours.

Loss and Bereavement

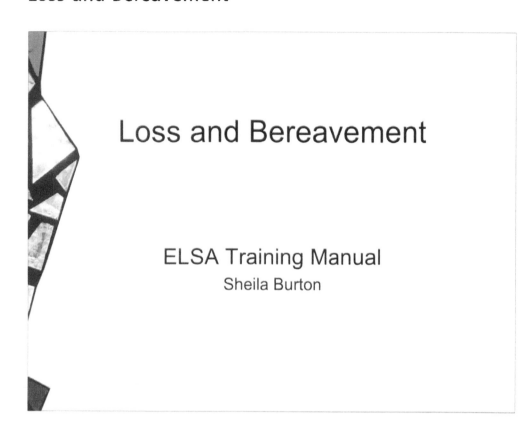

Aims

The aims are to:

- raise awareness of the extent of loss and bereavement in children's lives.
- consider the grieving process.
- understand the developmental nature of children's responses to death.
- increase ELSAs' confidence in supporting bereaved youngsters.

Facilitator Notes for Slide 2

This module will explore the range of loss that may impact on a child or young person's sense of wellbeing.

The nature of the grieving process will be considered, and two contrasting models of grief shared.

We will think about the different ways youngsters respond to death in relation to ages and stages of development.

There will be a strong focus on thinking about ways in which youngsters may be supported in school.

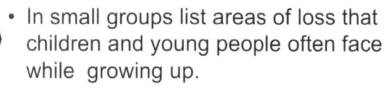

What is Loss?

- In small groups list areas of loss that children and young people often face while growing up.
- Think about the impact of some of these losses in your own childhood.

Activity Linked to Slide 3

The purpose of this slide is to help ELSAs consider the many significant losses, other than bereavement through death, that young people in school may experience.

Be aware that the invitation to be reflective may bring up difficult personal issues and therefore some uncomfortable feelings for participants.

Invite some feedback from participants.

Common Areas of Loss

- Familiar environments.
- Significant adults.
- Parental attention.
- Friendships.
- Opportunities.

Facilitator Notes for Slide 4

These are areas that may have been identified in the previous exercise.

Familiar Environments

Leaving nursery/playgroup, changing schools, moving home.

Significant Adults

Nursery staff, teachers, neighbours, departing parent/step-parent following relationship breakdown (1 in 5 experience parental divorce before the age of 16), death of a grandparent.

It has been estimated that at any one time, 70% of schools will be dealing with a recently bereaved child (Holland, 1993).

Parental Attention

Parent returning to work, grandparent requiring increased care, birth of new sibling, sibling with special needs, marital tensions, serious parental illness, other family crises such as unemployment or financial pressures.

Friendships

Break-up of friendships through conflict, moving home, school and so on.

Opportunities

Fear for children's safety causing reduced freedom to mix with peers outside school, curriculum pressure reducing opportunity to learn through free play in school, poverty reducing opportunity to experience leisure activities, holidays, travel, illness preventing an anticipated treat.

Unusual Loss

- Death of parent or sibling.
- Health (long-term illness or disability).
- Trust of adults (through abuse).
- Removal from family.
- Imprisonment of parent.

Facilitator Notes for Slide 5

A minority of children and young people will experience more extreme loss.

Death of Parent or Sibling

Approximately 5% of children aged 5-15 experience the death of a parent or sibling.

Health

A sudden catastrophic accident or illness.

Lifelong disability (physical or learning disability) limiting life opportunities.

Trust of Adults

Failure to form strong parental attachment.

Physical, sexual or emotional abuse.

Removal from Family

The degree of loss will be a function of the child's own perception of their need to be looked after outside of their birth family and of the circumstances surrounding being taken into care.

Imprisonment of Parent

A few children will experience long-term imprisonment of a parent as a result of serious crime, and may or may not have access to that parent.

Others will lose the presence of a parent for a shorter period of time, or repeatedly through their childhood.

Principles

- Grief is a normal reaction to loss.
- Most young people do not need grief counselling but need support.
- Young people are active in constructing their recovery from loss.
- Experience of loss is unique so the young person's perspective must be considered.
- A knowledge base of loss and bereavement is empowering to those giving support.

Facilitator Notes for Slide 6

Grief is normal, so normalising the process of grief for a bereaved young person is very helpful.

Grief counselling is not routinely needed, but should be considered if a young person seems to have become 'stuck' in the grief process. Normally what is needed is the support of family, friends and the school community.

Recovery from loss is an active process and it will be unique to each individual. Although there are likely to be common features, the uniqueness of every person's circumstances will create differences in the way they respond. It is therefore important to be attentive to the individual needs, thoughts and preferences of the youngster.

In the year 2000, around 7,500 young people (under 19) died prematurely through illness, accident or murder. This figure is indicative of the recurring incidence of personal tragedies. Most schools will therefore be confronted from time to time with the necessity of responding to such an event.

At this point it may be appropriate to pause for ELSAs to discuss any such experiences in their own schools and how they were managed.

Experiencing the death of someone close is almost certain to give rise to powerful emotions, the intensity of which may be unfamiliar to young people.

As professionals we can sometimes feel very uncomfortable and helpless in a situation where a colleague or young person has experienced a bereavement and may not know how to give appropriate support. Having awareness of the grief process and a range of support strategies empowers staff. It gives them the confidence to offer support to bereaved youngsters. It also helps them to recognise when a need for more specialised support arises.

The Grieving Process

Linear model with successive stages:

Shock (disbelief/denial)

⇩

Protest (at pain of separation)

⇩

Despair (guilt, anger, depression)

⇩

Acceptance (adjustment to new life)

Facilitator Notes for Slide 7

The grieving process has often been thought of as a linear model with the process taking up to two years, the first year (with its birthdays, celebrations and anniversaries) being the most traumatic.

The initial shock may be accompanied by disbelief and even denial. There can often be an initial numbness. Denial is the failure to acknowledge the absence by behaving as if the deceased were still there (for example, continuing to set a place at the table). This may last minutes only or persist for weeks.

The pain of separation may be shown by crying loudly or calling out for the dead loved one as if they could return.

With the growing awareness of the reality of loss may come a sense of despair. This can often be accompanied by guilt, anger and depression. There may be a strong need to seek understanding of the reason for the death and a need to visit where it happened.

There may be anger, which could be directed at anyone perceived to be at fault and even towards the deceased for leaving them.

The sadness and sense of emptiness can lead to depression.

Guilt is not uncommon. It may be expressed as, 'If only I had... been there/done more.' It may or may not be realistic. Perhaps the less realistic the guilt the more amenable it may be to reassurance. The realisation of the permanence of the loss may lead to extreme anxiety, even panic.

Acceptance allows the bereaved person to adjust to a changed life lived without their loved one and to find new ways of coping without them.

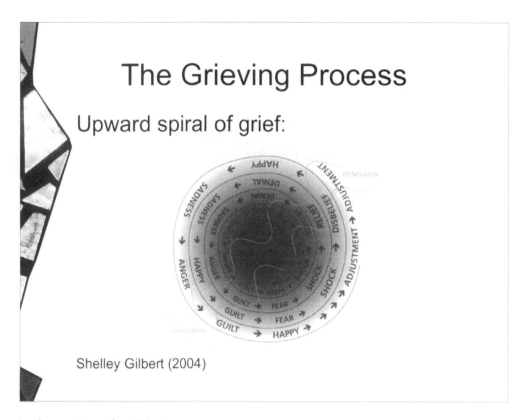

The Grieving Process

Upward spiral of grief:

Shelley Gilbert (2004)

Perhaps a more helpful model is *Shelley Gilbert's Upward Spiral of Grief* (2004).

This model treats the grieving process as a journey from an initial emotional black hole through an array of recurring feelings that become less intense as time goes on. They are the same feelings (shock, disbelief, denial, anger, guilt, fear) referred to in the linear model, but this model recognises that the feelings may be revisited several times. There is also recognition that these painful emotions can be punctuated by moments of happiness and laughter.

Such a mixture of emotions can feel enormously confusing and the bereaved youngster may feel they are going mad, which is why normalising their experiences is so important.

Changes in Behaviour

- What sort of changes might you expect to see (or have you seen) in bereaved youngsters?

- Discuss in small groups.

Activity Linked to Slide 9

This is an opportunity for ELSAs to think about how loss and grief might affect a young person.

Possible Behavioural Changes

- Increased emotionality and irritability.
- Social withdrawal, school refusal, friendship difficulties.
- Sleep difficulties.
- Headaches, stomach aches.
- Reduced concentration & attainment.
- Fear of being alone/separating from parent.
- Anxiety re: safety of self/others.
- Developmental regression.

Facilitator Notes for Slide 10

A grieving youngster may well show some of these changes in behaviour.

It's important to watch for these, as sometimes staff attribute the changes to other factors and dismiss bereavement as a root cause if there is a delay between the bereavement and the appearance of the changes.

Sometimes children appear to cope surprisingly well at the time but react later, when the initial attention has died down and they face the reality of changed circumstances.

Developmental Thinking

Children's responses to loss and death reflect their developmental stage of thinking.

- Babies and toddlers.
- Egocentric/magical thinking (3-7 years).
- Concrete thinking (7-11 years).
- Abstract thinking (11 years onwards).

Facilitator Notes for Slide 11

Babies will be influenced primarily by parents' emotional states and may be unsettled for a few weeks. Toddlers will not understand the permanence of death and may repeatedly ask about the deceased coming back. They may believe they did something wrong to cause the person to leave.

The ages suggested are only approximate guides and will vary from one child to another.

Young children are very egocentric in their thinking. They tend to see themselves as the centre of the universe and so believe their own wishes, thoughts and actions cause what happens to themselves and others.

The child may experience a compelling urge to recover the lost one (which fits in with their experience of fairy stories). They may think that if they are always good, endure bad things and wait for a long time the lost one will return.

They may become fearful that they themselves will die. They may react quite casually to the loss at first but then become upset or ask about loss/death at a later time.

The child may re-enact the cause of death or some aspect of it (for example, the funeral). This can be distressing for the adults but serves an important function for the child. Play is a means of understanding and integrating life's experiences.

From 7-11 years thinking tends to be quite black and white (either/or; good guys/bad guys).

Their capacity for subtlety, ambiguities or euphemisms is limited. Therefore phrases such as, 'We lost your sister,' 'Granny has gone to sleep,' 'Granddad is at rest,' can be confusing and frightening. In the latter part of this stage the permanence of death begins to be recognised. They also begin to realise that they themselves will die sometime.

By 11 or 12 a child is likely to perceive the finality of death in an adult way. At this age it is also easier for them to understand spiritual concepts of death.

Factors Affecting Children's Grief

- Age and development of thinking skills.
- Language skills.
- Quality of support.
- Context of loss or nature of death.
- Degree of attachment.
- Information made available.
- Control over events.
- Cultural/spiritual beliefs.

Facilitator Notes for Slide 12

Cognitive development is strongly influenced by language skills. Limitations in language skills influence understanding of the situation and also the expression of thoughts and feelings.

Good support assists healthy grieving.

The circumstances surrounding the loss or death will have a significant impact on the grieving process. People often report greater difficulty in adjusting to sudden and unexpected loss. In the case of death, murder or suicide, feelings of anger or guilt are likely to be even more intense. It is harder to make sense of the loss. Suicide will also bring with it a deep sense of rejection.

The degree of attachment to the departed person makes a difference to the process of recovery, as does the presence or absence of other strong attachment relationships. Whether the bereaved child has a secure attachment base will also be influential.

For young children views of death can often be distorted.

Death usually takes place away from home so there is an element of mystery.

Perceptions of death in the media are likely to produce an unreal picture.

Children may use the word 'kill' when describing death.

A fertile imagination about an unknown event may cause anxiety. Providing facts, sensitively managed (appropriate to the development of the particular child), is important.

We all need a sense of control over events. Including and taking account of the views of children and young people to an appropriate degree is supportive to the grieving process.

Those offering support need to be mindful of and sensitive towards the cultural practices and spiritual beliefs of the family.

Responding to Questions

- Don't brush them aside.
- Apply the Goldilocks Principle.
- Use language the child can understand.
- Avoid being shocked by blunt enquiry.
- Be sensitive to differing spiritual beliefs.

Facilitator Notes for Slide 13

Sometimes, for embarrassment or other reasons, we may want to brush aside children's questions. If they have been asked, they need an answer – even if it's an honest, 'I don't know.'

Apply the Goldilocks Principle – tell the child what they want to know, not too much and not too little.

Match your explanations to the developmental thinking and language skills of the child.

You may be asked some blunt questions about what happens to the body. This is not callous, but based on a need to understand.

Respect the family's or young person's beliefs though they may be different from your own. This is a time for support, not challenge. It is reasonable to acknowledge difference by using phrases like, 'Some people believe that…'. This is a useful approach to questions that don't have a definitive answer, such as, 'What is heaven like?' There are many different views, but nobody can be certain.

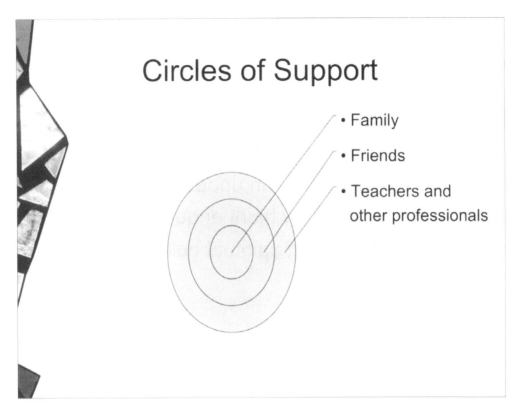

This model can help us think about who is supporting the bereaved so we can consider the level of response needed at any particular time. Each person's circle is different. Some draw support mainly from family or friends, some rely on religious groups and others prefer to obtain support from important adults in their life.

At home the parents may be struggling to manage their own grief let alone spending time listening to the child's grief. Sometimes children feel they cannot share their feelings with grieving parents in case they upset them further.

Friends may not have experienced grief so may not know how to support the child or young person.

Access to specialised counselling support may not be an immediate need post bereavement and in many cases may not be necessary at all. More important is access to supportive adults in school who can give the child or young person understanding and space to express their grief.

In complex circumstances such as suicide there may be a greater likelihood of need for specialist support, so referral to some kind of counselling service may be desirable. However this would not take away the need for someone to talk to in school as the need arises. Staff in school often worry about 'making it worse', which may lead them to withhold support, or at least to be in a dilemma about what best to do. But having knowledge about the grieving process, along with some simple support strategies, and do's and don'ts, can help staff feel empowered to offer support.

Often a student will prefer to talk to a known adult than to a stranger. It is recommended that such support is made available flexibly, when the student wants to talk. But it may also help to have a set time each week when the student knows they can go and talk to the adult in a set place. This should continue for as long as the young person wants it. ELSAs are well placed to offer this kind of support. Supporting a grieving youngster is emotionally demanding. It is important for ELSAs to have their own support in this work so that they do not become overwhelmed by the child's grief.

It is strongly advised that you don't undertake this work if you have been recently bereaved yourself. You need to be aware of any unresolved bereavement issues in your own life. The risk otherwise is that you fail to differentiate between your own grieving and that of the young person.

Complex Grief

- Suicide, murder, accidental death.
- Symptoms of post-trauma stress:
  - re-experiencing
  - avoidance
  - arousal.

Facilitator Notes for Slide 15

Any bereavement involving suicide, murder or accidental death may produce a more complex grieving process. If the bereaved witnesses the event, post-trauma symptoms may well occur. However, not everyone involved in a traumatic bereavement will require a high level of support. Their own resilience factors will affect their response.

Re-experiencing:

- Intense flashbacks.
- Intrusive thoughts and images that cause the incident to be relived.

Avoidance:

- Numbing of feelings.
- Refusal to think about the incident or people associated with it.
- A sense of distance from family and friends.
- Feelings of hopelessness about the future/futility of life.

Arousal:

- Difficulty sleeping.
- Volatility and irritability.
- Possible aggression.
- Inability to concentrate.
- Hyper-vigilance.

Supplementary Training

Supporting Loss

Discuss in small groups:

- What could the school do to help a young person experiencing loss?
- What part could you play?
- What areas of the curriculum could be used to explore loss?

Activity Linked to Slide 16

An ELSA is often the person the school community turns to when a young person has died or experienced the death of a close relative. They may be asked for ideas about how to manage the situation. They are also likely to be relied upon for direct support to pupils.

Helping Youngsters Express Grief

- The need to 'do' something.
- Writing letters and poems.
- Drawing pictures.
- Making a display.
- Sending off balloons.
- Lighting a candle.
- A memorial (for example, planting a tree).
- Memory box.

Facilitator Notes for Slide 17

The grieving process can be assisted by being able to do something.

If a classmate is bereaved, children may wish to send letters or make a card. If a classmate dies, they may want to write poems in memorial. These could be sent to the grieving family or could be used to make a display. They may also want to make a collection for flowers or other memorial.

Sending off helium-filled balloons, lighting a candle and tree planting are other ways that children can commemorate the loss of a friend. A space could be made available at school to commemorate a deceased pupil in the short term (a place to take flowers or messages). Sometimes a special garden area is created as a more lasting memorial.

A bereaved youngster may want to write a letter or poem to or about their friend or loved one to express the things they haven't been able to say in person.

A memorial assembly enables a corporate sharing of loss and celebration of a child's life.

Supporting the making of a memory box is a great way for an ELSA to help a bereaved youngster. Engaging in a practical activity gives the opportunity to talk, without requiring the youngster to do so until they are ready.

Some of the above ideas could be adapted for use with a young person who is experiencing the grief of a parent leaving the family home because of separation.

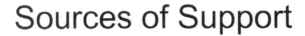

Sources of Support

- **Child Bereavement Network**
  www.childhoodbereavementnetwork.org.uk
- **Child Bereavement Trust**
  www.childbereavement.org.uk
- **Winston's Wish**
  www.winstonswish.org.uk
- **Cruse Bereavement Care**
  www.crusebereavementcare.org.uk & www.rd4u.org.uk
- **Compassionate Friends**
  www.tcf.org.uk
- **Simon Says**
  www.simonsays.org.uk

Facilitator Notes for Slide 18

These websites are useful sources of information and ideas for support. Some provide resources that can be used in school.

References

Argyle, M. (1987) 'Some New Developments in Social Skills Training', in Mayor B. M. & Pugh A. K. (eds) *Language, Communication and Education*. London: Croom Helm.

Asperger, H. (1944) 'Autistic Psychopathy' in Childhood was first published as "Die autistischen Psychopathen in Kindesalter in Archiv fur Psychiatrie und Nervenkrankemheiten" main citation is Uta Frith (1991)'. *Autism and Asperger Syndrome*.

Attwood, A. J., Frith, U. & Hermelin, B. (1988) The understanding and use of interpersonal gestures by Autistic and Down's Syndrome children, *Journal of Autism and Developmental Disorders*, Vol. 18.

Bagshaw, M. (2000) *Using Emotional Intelligence at Work*. Ely: Fenman Ltd. *Journal of Abnormal and Social Psychology*, 63, 575-582.

Bandura, A., Ross, D. & Ross, S. A. (1961) 'Transmission of aggression through imitation of aggressive models'. *Journal of Abnormal and Social Psychology*, Vol. 63, pp. 575-582.

Baron-Cohen, S., Leslie, A. M. & Frith, U. (1985) 'Does the autistic child have a "theory of mind"?' *Cognition*, 21, 37-46.

Baron-Cohen, S. (1989) The autistic child's theory of mind: the case of specific developmental delay. *Journal of Child Psychology and Psychiatry*, 30: 285-98.

Berne, E. (1975) *Transactional Analysis in Psychotherapy*. London: Souvenir Press.

Borba, M. (1989) *Esteem Builders' Complete Programme*. Torrance, CA: Jalmar Press.

Bradshaw, M. (2000) *Using Emotional Intelligence at Work*. Ely: Fenman Ltd.

Breakwell, G. M. (1997) *Coping with Aggressive Behaviour*. Leicester: British Psychological Society.

Brett, D. (1986) *Annie Stories*. New York: Workman Publishing.

Burton, S. (2008) 'Empowering learning support assistants to enhance the emotional wellbeing of children in school'. *Educational & Child Psychology*, 25(2), 40-56.

Cowen, E. L., Pederson, A., Babigian, H. & Izzo, L. D. (1973) 'Long-term follow-up of early detected vulnerable children'. *Journal of Consulting and Clinical Psychology*. Vol. 41.

Elkins, D. P. (ed) (1976) *Glad to be Me*. Englewood Cliffs, NJ: Prentice Hall.

Faupel, A., Herrick, E. & Sharp, P. (1998) *Anger Management: A Practical Guide*. London: David Fulton Publishers.

Frederickson, N. (2002). Evidence-based practice and educational psychology. *Educational and Child Psychology*, Vol. 19

Frith, U. (1989) *Autism: Explaining the enigma*. Oxford: Blackwell.

Gardner, H. (1983) *Frames of Mind: the theory of multiple intelligences*. New York: Basic Books.

Georgiades, N. J. & Phillimore, L. (1975 'The myth of the hero-innovator' in *Behaviour Modification with the Severely Retarded*. In C. C. Kiernan & F. P. Woodford (eds) *Behaviour Modification with the Severely Retarded*. Amsterdam: Associated Scientific Publishers.

Gilbert, S. (2004) *Grief Encounter: A workbook to encourage conversations between children and adults*. London: National Children's Bureau.

Goleman, D. (1995) *Emotional Intelligence*. New York: Bantam Books.

Goleman, D. (1998) *Working with Emotional Intelligence*. New York: Bantam Books.

Gordon, J. & Grant, G. (eds) (1997) *How We Feel: An Insight into the Emotional World of Teenagers*. London: Jessica Kingsley.

Gray, C., Arnold, S. & Pauken, S. A. (revised edn) (2001) *The New Social Story Book*. Arlington, TX: Future Horizons Incorporated.

Hutchings, S., Comins, J. & Offiler, J. (1991) *The Social Skills Handbook*. Bicester: Winslow Press.

Kanner, L. (1943) 'Autistic disturbances of affective contact'. *Nervous Child*, 2, 217-250.

Loomans, D. & Loomans, J. (1994) *Full Esteem Ahead: One hundred ways to teach values and build self-esteem for all ages*. Tuberton, California: Kramer.

Maines, B. (2002) *Children Can Learn with their Shoes Off: Supporting young people with Asperger's Syndrome in mainstream schools and colleges*. London: Paul Chapman Publishing, A Lucky Duck Book.

Maslow, A. H. (1987) *Motivation and Personality* (3rd ed) New York: Harper & Rowe.

Mayer, J. D. & Salovey, P. (1997) What is emotional intelligence? In P. Salovey & D. Sluyter (eds) *Emotional Development and Emotional Intelligence: Implications for Educators* (pp. 3-31) New York: Basic Books.

Newton, C., Taylor, G. & Wilson, C. (1996) Circles of Friends: An inclusive approach to meeting emotional and behavioural needs. *Educational Psychology in Practice*, 11 (4) 41-48.

Park, J. (2000) 'The Dance of Dialogue: Thinking and Feeling in Education'. *The Journal for Pastoral Care & Personal/Social Education*, Vol. 18 (3), pp. 11–15.

Pearpoint, J., Forest, M. & Snow, J. (1992) *The Inclusion Papers: Strategies to make inclusion work*. Toronto: Inclusion Press.

Pope, A. W. (1988) 'The Five-scale Test of Self-esteem for Children: Junior and Secondary', in A. W. Pope, S. M. Mchale & W. E. Craighead (eds), *Self-esteem enhancement with children and adolescents*. Oxford: Pergamon Press.

Carol Rowe (1999) 'Do social stories benefit children with autism in mainstream primary schools?' *British Journal of Special Education*, Vol. 26, No. 1, pp12-14.

Sainsbury, C. (2000) *Martian in the Playground*. Bristol: Lucky Duck Publishing.

Salovey, P. & Mayer, J. D. (1990) 'Emotional Intelligence'. *Imagination, Cognition and Personality*, 9, 185-211.

Schutz, W. (1998) 'The Interpersonal World' in Adler, R. B. & Rodman, G. (eds). *Understanding Human Communication* (3rd ed) London: Holt, Reinhart & Winston.

Sharp, P. (2001) *Nurturing Emotional Literacy: A practical guide for teachers, parents and those in the caring professions*. London: David Fulton Publishers.

References

Shotton, G. (1998) 'A circle of friends approach with socially neglected children'. *Educational Psychology in Practice*, Vol. 14, No. 2.

Shotton, G. & Burton, S. (2008) *Emotional Wellbeing: An Introductory Handbook*. London: Optimus Education.

Sinclair, J. (1993) 'Don't mourn for us.' *Our Voice*, Vol. 1, No. 3.

Smith, C. (2003) *Writing and Developing Social Stories*. Milton Keynes: Speechmark Publishing.

Whitehouse, E. & Pudney, W. (1996) *A Volcano in My Tummy*. Gabriola Island, BC: New Society Publishers.

Wimmer, H. & Perner, J. (1983) 'Second Bisontine Conference for Conceptual and Linguistic Development in the Child Aged from 1 to 6 Years' (later called the Sally-Anne test).

Wing, L. (1981) 'Language, social, and cognitive impairments in autism and severe mental retardation'. *Journal of Autism and Developmental Disorders*, Vol. 11, No. 1.

Wolff, S., Narayan, S. & Moyes, B. (1988) 'Personality characteristics of parents of autistic children: A controlled study'. *Journal of Child Psychology and Psychiatry*, Vol. 29.

www.mentalhealth.org.uk/media/news-releases/news-releases-2004/25-october-2004/